Books of Light

To All Who Write,
And As They Write,
Bring in New Light
For Us To See By.

Books of Light

*A Compilation of Reviews
of Outstanding Books in the Fields
of Science Fiction, Metaphysics,
Holistic Health, and the Esoteric*

**by the Editors
of Books of Light Book Club**

ARIEL PRESS
Columbus, Ohio

Third Edition

This book is made possible
by gifts to the Publications Fund of Light

Books of Light
Copyright © 1986, 1988, 1991 by Light

All Rights Reserved. No part of this book may be used or reproduced in any manner whatever without written permission, except in the case of brief quotations embodied in articles and reviews. Printed in the United States of America. Direct inquiries to: Ariel Press, 3854 Mason Road, Canal Winchester, Ohio 43110.

ISBN 0-89804-155-4

Contents

Preface — 11
Books of Light — 19
Exploring The Tarot — 21
I Say Sunrise — 22
The Reappearance of the Christ — 23
Kinship With All Life — 24
No One Hears But Him — 25
Winged Pharaoh — 27
Divine Healing of Mind and Body — 30
Esoteric Philosophy of Love & Marriage — 31
Clairvoyant Investigations — 33
The Impersonal Life — 34
Narcissus & Goldmund — 35
Active Meditation — 36
The Bach Flower Remedies — 39
The Tao of Meow — 40
War in Heaven — 42
Myth Conceptions — 43
Health and Light — 44
The New View Over Atlantis — 45
A Whack on the Side of the Head — 49
Glory Road — 51
Across the Unknown — 52
Initiation — 53
The Fountainhead — 54

5

The Mind Parasites — 55
The Earthsea Trilogy — 59
There is a River — 62
Healing & Regeneration Through Color &
       Music — 63
A Soul's Journey — 64
Prodigal Genius — 67
The Secret Teachings of All Ages — 68
A**hole No More! — 70
The Practice of the Presence of God — 71
Siddhartha — 72
Saga of the Well World — 73
Explore Your Psychic World — 76
The Great Divorce — 77
Forces of the Zodiac — 79
The Initiation of the World — 81
The Unfinished Autobiography — 82
Childhood's End — 83
The Power of the Rays & Colour
       Meditations — 84
The Hidden Side of Things — 85
An Encyclopedia of Traditional Symbols — 89
God Always Says Yes — 91
The Time Quartet — 92
Scars of the Soul — 95
The Hour Glass — 98
The World of Null-A — 100

The Players of Null-A — 101
Magister Ludi — 102
Your Power To Be — 103
The Spiritual Fitness Handbook — 104
Stranger in a Strange Land — 105
Occult Medicine Can Save Your Life — 106
Far Memory — 107
The Pleasantries of the Incredible Mulla
      Nasrudin — 109
A Sampling of Nasrudin — 110
The Call to the Heights — 111
The Secret Path — 112
The Boy Who Saw True — 113
The Chronicles of Narnia — 116
Driving Your Own Karma — 118
The Secret Life of the Unborn Child — 119
And the Devil Will Drag You Under — 122
The Secrets of Dr. Taverner — 123
Thought-Forms — 124
From Bethlehem to Calvary — 125
The Brotherhood of Angels and Men — 127
The Sea Priestess — 130
OM, The Secret of Ahbor Valley — 131
In Search of the New Age — 135
Memories, Dreams, & Reflections — 137
The Greater Trumps — 138
Reincarnation — 141

Life as Carola — 142
The Dragonriders of Pern — 143
Practical Mysticism — 144
The Chakras & the Human Energy
   Fields — 146
Return to Elysium — 149
The Betty Book — 150
The Arthurian Saga — 151
The Nine Billion Names of God — 152
After We Die, What Then? — 153
Fart Proudly — 155
The Powers of Thought — 156
Atlas Shrugged — 159
Esoteric Christianity — 160
The Fullness of Human Experience — 163
King—of the Khyber Rifles — 165
The Twelve Powers of Man — 166
Moon Magic — 167
The Light Within Us — 168
Visible Light — 169
The Inner Life — 171
Waldo & Magic, Inc. — 174
The Seven Human Temperaments — 175
Edgar Cayce's Story of Attitudes
   & Emotions — 176
Great Lion of God — 177
The Book of Runes — 179

The Real World of Fairies — 182
The Space Trilogy — 183
Eyes of Horus — 186
Lord of the Horizon — 187
The Magic Kingdom of Landover — 188
Edgar Cayce on Reincarnation — 191
The Story of the Other Wise Man — 193
90 Days to Self-Health — 194
Scarlet Feather — 195
I Ching On Line — 196
The Place of the Lion — 197
Dance Band on the Titanic — 198
The Unobstructed Universe — 199
The Philosopher's Stone — 200
The Winged Bull — 201
The Gift of Healing — 203
The Screwtape Letters — 204
Masters and Men — 205
The Razor's Edge — 206
Lord of Light — 207
Assignment in Eternity — 208
A Search in Secret India — 209
The Autobiography of a Yogi — 210
Job: A Comedy of Justice — 212
The Four Lords of the Diamond — 213
The Apprentice Adept — 214
Bestselling Titles — 216

Acquiring These Books

Many of these books are readily available in large bookstores; some will be easily found in libraries as well. This is especially true of the science fiction and popular fiction. But a substantial number of the books reviewed in this volume are not widely distributed and can be quite hard to find. Perhaps the appearance of this bibliography will inspire more stores and libraries to add these titles.

As this book goes to press, however, all of these books are presently in print and are available through Books of Light. Books of Light is a book club with a difference. It makes available a wide selection of inspired books. Yet members are never under any pressure to purchase books.

No books are ever sent automatically; only those which members specifically order are sent.

For current prices and availability of any of these books, just write to Books of Light, 3854 Mason Road, Canal Winchester, Ohio 43110. Or call toll free (in Canada as well as the U.S.): 1-800-336-7769.

Preface

This little book is meant to be a doorway into a new dimension. It is a collection of reviews of books that are featured in the Books of Light book club. Reading these reviews is not the same as reading the books themselves. But if you read one of these reviews and are inspired to read the book, then you have opened the door and passed into the next dimension.

It is a very special dimension, too, filled with magic and mystery, love and goodwill, joy and laughter, adventure and triumph, struggle and growth, wisdom and insight. It is a dimension that will stretch your mind and exercise your imagination. It will open up new mental horizons, and reveal new possibilities you have never dreamed of before. It will challenge your self-honesty, and if you pass the test, it will lay the groundwork for real transformation and genuine spiritual growth.

This is an inner dimension, reached by reading and thinking. But not by reading any old book. The books reviewed in this small volume have all been chosen because of their unusual capacity to introduce us to some facet of our inner life and potential to grow.

Books of Light is a special kind of book club. The titles we feature must radiate the light of intelligence, or we do not select them. To qualify for our club, a book must help us, one way or another, become more aware of the inner potential of our humanity and show us what to do with it. This is no small order. Many writers claim to be inspired, but their words lack light. It is rare to find a writer who truly is inspired by his or her inner self, the inner dimensions of life. When we do find such writers, we should celebrate their talent and applaud their accomplishments. This is the purpose of this collection. It is not a collection of critiques, but of reviews. It praises creativity and genius, instead of finding fault with it. It is meant to open doors.

This book contains reviews of both fiction and nonfiction. The fiction tends to be mostly fantasy and science fiction, although there are some outstanding exceptions to this general rule—the novels of Joan Grant, Taylor Caldwell, Charles Williams, and Dion Fortune, to name a few. Many people shy away from fiction, because they think "it's not true." This is a tragic misunderstanding. Good fiction often reveals and describes to us the nature of the inner dimensions of life far more powerfully than any stuffy treatise. In fact, many of the novels chosen for review in this collection are veritable textbooks on one aspect of the inner life or another. Colin Wilson's *The Mind Parasites*, for instance, gives a far more lucid account of psychic attack than any nonfiction book. Ursula LeGuin's masterpiece, *The Earthsea Trilogy*, tells us far more about the process of overcoming the dark elements within ourselves—and radiates more light in the process—than almost any book on metaphysics or personal transformation. Certainly Anne McCaffrey's *Dragonriders of Pern* series teaches us more about the true workings of the subconscious than any college text on psychology!

The nonfiction that we feature embraces many categories, from holistic healing to psychic phenomena, from metaphysics to meditation, from autobiography to the arcane, and from the creative to the cosmic. Nonfiction titles range from *Exploring the Tarot* to *A Whack on the Side of the Head*, from *Active Meditation* to *Practical Mysticism*, from *The New View Over Atlantis* to *The Powers of Thought*. We do not promote any enshrined viewpoint in choosing these titles, save one. Each book must lead us to a greater understanding and awareness of light—the light within us.

What is this light? Answering this question is part of the fun and adventure of reading these books. In brief, however, we can state that it is the light within great ideas—the light which inspires these authors to write their books, and the light which fills us with new ideas and fresh insights as we read them. In a magical way, reading is meant to be an act of sharing and communion, as we interact with the same ideas and inner realities which first inspired the book.

The perceptive reader will quickly discover what this means. Something alchemical occurs as we read these books. They inspire us to new aspiration and new achievement. They enrich our thinking. There is a living presence in each of these books, and as we interact with this living presence, new doors in consciousness open to us, awaiting our exploration.

Our intent is to help you open some of these doors. In no way do we mean to suggest that the following set of reviews is a complete bibliography of the best books in these fields. Such a list would be almost impossible to compile. So we have imposed a few limitations. First, all of these books are presently in print. We have purposefully excluded out of print books, no matter how inspired, simply because a book which cannot be read cannot open any doors!

The second limitation is an even more practical one. We have only included books we have actually featured in the book club. There are many excellent books which will be selected as the club continues to serve its members; these books will be included in future editions. C.W. Leadbeater was represented in the first edition of this collection, for instance, only by his book *Thought-Forms*, even though he is one of our favorite authors. In this third edition, several of his books are reviewed. What made the difference? Quite simply, the books became available again. At the same time, some books included in the first two editions have been dropped from this one.

Undoubtedly, there will be many people who take exception with our choices. They will wonder why specific authors are not included, especially if they have found them particularly inspirational. "Just what is your criteria for including and excluding books?" they will demand. This is an unanswerable question, for we have no formula, except that a book radiate light. But there are some types of books which we do not and will not promote:

• Those which espouse the use of drugs as a means to the expansion of consciousness or enlightenment. No matter how fascinating these accounts might be, they do not lead us toward the light. They promote only silliness and irresponsibility.

• The "wow wonderful" type of book, in which the author suddenly discovers proof of life after death, reincarnation, or psychic communication. Such books play an important role, of course, but all of these phenomena have been documented so many times in the past that the "new revelation" begins to tire, except for people who have never considered such ideas before. In selecting our titles, we assume that our members have some acquaintance with these ideas and want to be stimulated by important new thoughts, not just convinced of their integrity and truthfulness.

• The "wow wonderful" type of book by celebrities. Famous people are often very helpful in spreading exotic ideas and making the average person more comfortable with them. But just having a famous name does not make anyone more enlightened, or more knowledgeable, than anyone else.

• Books capitalizing on popular fads. Enlightenment is measured neither by popularity nor by current fashion. We do not think we really need another book on how to jog your way to nirvana, how to become clairvoyant while you sleep, or how the Chernobyl disaster was caused by the misapplication of psychic energy by secret Russian mediums. If we wanted to be amused in this way, we would rather watch an old Marx brothers' movie.

• Imitations. Imitation is undoubtedly the sincerest form of flattery, but it is not usually worth much. Unfortunately, the fields of metaphysics and psychic discovery are flooded by cheap imitations. There are, for example, at least a dozen books out on color therapy, yet none compare with the very first ones written on the subject by S.G.J. Ouseley. That is why we feature his books, not the imitations. The market is also flooded with books about the Tarot, yet only one, *Exploring the Tarot* by Carl Japikse, measures up to our standards. So that is the one we carry.

• Wolves in sheep's clothing. Many books are written which claim to deal with holistic healing or psychic discoveries, yet fail to reveal anything genuine of the inner life. Instead, their treatment is very superficial, and their recommendations are highly influenced by materialistic assumptions. A good example of this is any book which recommends vegetarianism as a spiritual practice. It is what we feed our minds and inner self that determine our progress toward enlightenment, not what we feed our physical bodies. No one yet has ever eaten his or her way to heaven.

In short, we have made a conscious effort to sift through and discard the cheap, the shabby, and the phony. Each of the books reviewed in this volume is a treasure. There are no ringers.

Yet many people will pick up these treasures and fail to recognize them for what they are. No doors will open. They will not tap the light within the words. They may even dismiss the words as "silly" or "impractical" or "nonsense."

How can this happen? It can happen because there is an art to reading inspired literature, be it fiction or nonfiction. It is not enough just to read the words; we must also try to read the thoughts behind the words—the light or creative idea which originally inspired the author. Reading is meant to be an act of transcendence, where the power of the words lifts us up to a higher level of perception than we normally enjoy. But this can only happen if we are making the effort to read intelligently.

In reading nonfiction, we should do more than just try to absorb new facts. Filling our mind with facts prepares us only for trivia contests and cocktail parties. Facts have their place, but they are just the outer flesh of the inner idea. In reading, therefore, we must try to understand the basic ideas, not just facts. Even more importantly, we must take the most significant of these ideas and integrate them into our values, ethics, attitudes, goals, and character.

Reading about reincarnation is a good example of this principle. The average person loves to read about the vivid details of earlier lives of specific people, for this sets in motion speculation about his or her own previous lives, leading quickly to glamorous fantasies and unrealistic play-acting. None of this is productive thinking. The intelligent person, by contrast, will try to use the facts and examples of reincarnation that he or she reads about to stimulate mature contemplation about the archetypal processes of rebirth, accountability, and transformation. In this way, the magical act of reading opens up new doors—not just alluring blind alleys.

In reading fiction, we should do more than just escape into an absorbing story. Inspired fiction is usually highly symbolic; the plot unfolds on several levels all at once. There is the literal level of the story line, but there is also the hidden level of esoteric symbolism. The novel *Glory Road* by Robert Heinlein is a good example of this. On the literal level, it may seem to some people to be little more than a somewhat gory adventure story spiced with sex. Symbolically, however, a wholly different story unfolds, as we see the adventures of the hero as the struggles of the aspirant on the spiritual path. There is great wisdom in this novel, yet the average reader might easily read the whole novel without grasping its insights and meanings at all.

These books demand that we stretch our thinking and imagination. If we are satisfied with what we know already, these books may well offend us. But if we hunger for more insight into life, these books will nourish us. They will nurture us with light.

No one's life ever needs to be dull, one dimensional. The rich treasures of inspired reading are available to us all, if only we will avail ourselves of them. Whether you are new to the world of enlightened books, or a confirmed student of the arcane, the treasure awaits.

Books of Light

From the Aquarian Tarot

Exploring the Tarot
by Carl Japikse

There are few things in life more plentiful than books on the Tarot. Unfortunately, none of them has been worth reading.

Until now. Carl Japikse's new book, *Exploring the Tarot,* is not just the definitive book on the Tarot, but it is likely to revolutionize the use of this ancient tool of divination as well.

Mr. Japikse decries the use of the Tarot as a fortune telling device, and explains that its true function is to act as a means for interacting with the divine archetypes that shape life. For this reason, he proposes using the Tarot as an integral part of what he calls the process of self-examination—the work of exploring our values, beliefs, habits, and attitudes and how they have been shaped.

By pursuing this theme, Mr. Japikse skillfully reveals the true dynamics and potential of the Tarot, as though he were carefully peeling away layer after layer of soot and grime from an old painting and revealing a splendid masterpiece for all to see.

While making it clear that it is not his intention to give a list of interpretations for the cards in the Tarot deck, he does present a structure by which each reader can build his or her own associations with the Tarot symbols. He also presents a number of humorous demonstrations of what it means to interact intuitively with the Tarot.

The book concludes with transcripts from five actual Tarot readings.

There is no better book on the Tarot.

I Say Sunrise
by Talbot Mundy

"The world is visibly moving from bad to worse, if we can trust our senses. But can we trust senses that lie to us about such ordinary everyday occurrences as sunrise and sunset?"

Talbot Mundy says no, and encourages us to go forward to the beginning—the sunrise—of life, and awaken not our senses, but our consciousness. He challenges us to discover, and prove to ourselves, that joy *is* stronger than sorrow, love *is* stronger than hatred, hope *is* stronger than despair, energy *is* stronger than sloth, and good *is* stronger than evil.

I Say Sunrise is a joyous book, all the more remarkable because the joy that fills its pages was cultivated, the author reports, in the face of great struggle, shame, and grief. On the surface, *I Say Sunrise* is a statement of Talbot Mundy's philosophy of life, a metaphysical classic. But beneath the surface, it is more than this alone. It teaches us how to fill life with joy, so that we can triumph over struggle, shame, and grief, too.

It is also a direct assault on the limitations of mass consciousness, describing how the popular beliefs of society color individual thinking, and what we can do to reclaim proprietorship over our own convictions and attitudes. Along the way, there are chapters on death, reincarnation, the use of money, love, and prayer.

This is a powerful book; it awakens us from sleep. As Mundy writes: "What is beyond the darkness? Some say chaos and darker night. I Say Sunrise."

The Reappearance of the Christ

by Alice A. Bailey

Ever since Jesus walked the earth and set forth His teachings of peace and goodwill, men and women have longed for His return. Many have prophesied His return at a specific time and place, attracting the interest of others, only to be disappointed by the absence of a physical appearance. What we have forgotten is that the Christ, Who is spirit, has never left us; He has always been with us. Instead of cultivating a better rapport with the spiritual reality of the Christ, we have hoped for the reappearance of the exact physical form of Jesus.

In *The Reappearance of the Christ*, Alice Bailey takes humanity to task for its failure to cultivate an ongoing relationship with the living Christ, falling instead into an almost useless worship of a crucified Jesus. She paints a fascinating picture of just how active the Christ has been, not only throughout the ages but more importantly in our modern age—working behind the scenes, to be sure, from the inner levels, but nonetheless as the most important influence on the evolution of humanity.

She goes on to outline the changes we need to make in our thinking and action to establish right rapport with the Christ and allow Him—and the Hierarchy as a whole—to reappear physically and interact openly with humanity.

The Reappearance of the Christ is one of the most readable and important of all the books Alice Bailey wrote. It is highly recommended.

Kinship With All Life
by J. Allen Boone

The human race does not inhabit the planet earth alone. We share it with many kingdoms of life. Yet we often have little appreciation for the value of these other kingdoms.

As a race, we desperately need a larger perspective on life. We need to cultivate a deeper reverence for all life and see the kingdoms that inhabit the earth—animal, plant, and mineral—as worthy expressions of the One Creator.

J. Allen Boone's remarkable book, *Kinship with all Life*, is a charming introduction to the true meaning of reverence. It is the story of Boone's personal experiences with animals, how he learned to communicate with them, and the respect and love he has developed for them.

The principal figure of the book is Strongheart, a famous movie dog of his day. Asked to care for Strongheart while his trainers were away, Boone readily consented. However, he soon began having second thoughts, as Strongheart seemed far more capable of taking care of Boone than the other way around! As he got to know the famous dog, Boone marveled at his range of intelligence—and found he could communicate telepathically with him.

These experiences led Boone to explore contacts with other animals, too—rattlesnakes, ants, and "Freddie the Fly." His observations and insights make fascinating and entertaining reading, and put a unique and practical focus on the concept of reverence for life.

This book is a joy to read.

No One Hears But Him
by Taylor Caldwell

"For all the talk of 'love' there is in the world today the fact remains that never has the world been so absolutely loveless, hard of heart, murderous, cruel, rejecting, contemptuous, and indifferent. Never has the heart of man been so faithless as the heart of modern man, for all the babble of 'involvement' and 'concern for humanity.'"

Wanting to see this change, Taylor Caldwell has written a novel of unusual power—a novel which can help us make this change ourselves. *No One Hears But Him* is the story of a great sanctuary, located in a park in a large city. In this sanctuary waits The Man Who Listens. He waits for the angry, the hopeless, the cynical, the bereaved, and the burdened to come and tell Him their story, so they may be healed.

The Man Who Listens hears but does not speak. But as these angry, hopeless people tell of their troubles and rage, a powerful change begins to occur within them. Sometimes they hear a voice within them, speaking quiet counsel; sometimes they have an inner vision. In some cases, the change is not dramatic at all. But they begin to understand themselves and what they can do to take control of their lives, and they leave the sanctuary uplifted, with fresh wisdom and poise.

The Man Who Listens, of course, is the Christ—the Christ within us who can speak to us and guide us, if we will only listen. Few novels contain a greater power for transformation than this one. It should be read by all.

Winged Pharaoh
by Joan Grant

Outstanding fiction always has the capacity to conjure a setting and a time, and make the reader feel that he or she is right there, absorbing the flavor of the surroundings and participating in the action. Few novels, however, succeed in doing this as well as Joan Grant's classic story of ancient Egypt, *Winged Pharaoh*.

First published in 1937 but difficult to obtain in recent years, *Winged Pharaoh* is something far greater than the usual stories of vanity and intrigue found in cheap romances about Egypt. Revolving around the story of a young princess who becomes an initiate of the occult teachings of the time and then a "winged Pharaoh" in the first dynasty of ancient Egypt, this is a glorious novel, an epic in enlightened living. It provides a masterful glimpse into an era and culture which has been all but lost to history.

Sekhet-a-ra is the daughter of the Pharaoh and destined to become, with her brother Neyah, co-ruler of Kam, as Egypt was called in those times. As a child, she develops a strong love for the teachings of the mystery schools, fascinated by the stories told her by her father and Ptah-kefer, the high priest.

While still young, Sekhet-a-ra, or Sekeeta, as she is usually called, begins having psychic experiences of her own and is recognized as one who will be, with proper training, a "winged Pharaoh"—a ruler and priest with clairvoyant powers. At the age of ten, she is sent to the temple school for rigorous training in esoteric knowledge and the development of her inner powers and awareness.

Much of the book is devoted to describing this training and the nature of the mysteries. For the reader who is interested in the psychic aspects of life, the principles of intelligent living, and the natural unfoldment of the spiritual life, these passages hold great keys to understanding. Indeed, they are written with such clarity, detail, and living presence that it is quite reasonable to believe, as Joan Grant has stated, that her story was really a "far memory" and not a work of fiction at all—an actual recollection and reconstruction of life in ancient Egypt.

Sekeeta's training concludes with a detailed account of her four days of initiation, during which time she is out of her body and facing powerful tests of her will and discernment. She is then ready to handle the challenges of being priestess and Pharaoh.

It is not possible to read this book without being struck by the realization that the ancient Egyptians were often far wiser in their approach to life than we are in modern society. They viewed dreams, for example, as out-of-body experiences of learning or service, and Sekeeta is given training to remember her dreams more clearly. As she progresses, she also finds she can be taught by discarnate teachers as well as her physical ones.

Sekeeta learns the mysteries of life after death, too. "We are all travelers upon a long journey, as we pass through many countries. We may find gardens and tranquil rivers where for a time we are happy; yet in our hearts, we know we are exiles and long to return to our true home." The journey, of course, is the time spent on earth; the true home is the inner life of spirit.

The person who craves salacious accounts of the court life of the Pharaohs may be disappointed by this story. But for the intelligent reader, *Winged Pharaoh* is a rare delight, a rich introduction to the cosmology, culture, healing arts, and psychic life of Egypt.

Today, as the mysteries of life are being restored to earth, the hidden and esoteric practices of 'Kam' provide us with a clue of what is to come in our society, as spirit once more dominates our culture and thinking. What was known to only a few priests in Egypt may, one day, become common knowledge to the whole of science, for the good of mankind.

Winged Pharaoh is an important book.

Divine Healing of Mind and Body
by Murdo MacDonald-Bayne

"The world is still eating of the fruit of the Tree of Knowledge of Good and Evil, and only when mankind takes hold of the Tree of Life—the Christ within—will his salvation come."

Taking hold of the Christ within and learning to use its power to heal the mind and the body is the theme of one of our age's most remarkable books, a transcription of 14 lectures delivered by Jesus through Dr. Murdo MacDonald-Bayne during the year 1948.

At the start of each lecture, the power and intelligence of the Master would take control of the body of MacDonald-Bayne and speak flawlessly about a topic of spiritual growth.

But the mechanics of how these lectures were given are not nearly as important as the peace, love, and illumination of the words recorded in this book. For *Divine Healing of Mind and Body* stands by itself, without claims and affidavits, as a series of brilliant insights into human and divine nature, prayer, and faith.

This is the sort of book which we can open at random, and no matter what we read, come away inspired and refreshed. When read from cover to cover, however, the ideas in this book become a magical presence which fills our thinking and awareness with beauty, reverence, love, and new insights.

There is great power, intelligence, truth, and healing in this book. It is highly recommended to all who seek to know God.

Esoteric Philosophy of Love & Marriage
by Dion Fortune

The subjects of sexual love and marriage are important ones to most people, but are also subjects which have been shrouded in mystery, dogma, guilt, confusion, and rumor. The person seeking to honor the higher principles of life often struggles greatly with these issues, without satisfactory resolution.

This book by Dion Fortune is one of the best statements in print regarding sexual love and marriage. It seeks to put the many areas of confusion regarding these issues into an esoteric perspective. As such, it considers sex to be one of the energies of life and self-expression, no more or less divine than any other energy. Like all energies of life, it must be used with respect, purpose, and self-control, or it will go awry—but it *is* an important, healthy, and creative element of human life.

In order to develop fully this basic theme, Miss Fortune begins with a brief examination of the esoteric doctrine of energy and its manifestation in consciousness and matter. This short summary alone makes the book worthwhile, but it is actually just an introduction to her real topics: the esoteric concept of sex, the ideal marriage, the interplay of male and female polarities, and the creative potentials arising from a balanced use of these energies.

Esoteric Philosophy of Love and Marriage is an important book, highly recommended to all who want to understand the principles of life.

Clairvoyant Investigations
by Geoffrey Hodson

Geoffrey Hodson was one of the truly great clairvoyants of the twentieth century. This new book was one of his final projects—and it is a fitting culmination to a distinguished career.

Hodson picks two of his favorite themes for further clairvoyant investigation—the angelic kingdom and the power of music. After a brief introduction to both subjects, he goes on to describe in great detail his clairvoyant observations and their significance. In many cases, these observations are complemented by stunning color illustrations of what Hodson saw psychically.

In the section on angels, Hodson carefully documents the interaction of angels of various grades with the forces of nature, with the vital energy of the earth, with solar energy, and with the healing of humanity. But he does not just describe what he "sees," as fascinating as this is—he also describes the inner depths of consciousness in these angelic powers. As such, there is much we can learn about our own consciousness.

In the section on music, Hodson examines the forces and forms set in motion by the performance of music by humans, the angelic beings this attracts, and the impact of music on our own consciousness. Perhaps the most fascinating observations are those dealing with the effect of holy music, although the pieces he examines range from "Greensleeves" to Bach.

Clairvoyant Investigations is a beautifully illustrated book with a powerful presence.

The Impersonal Life

Within each of us, there is a central divine essence which is the *real self*. Few of us recognize this inner self, however. Instead, we identify with our physical body, our thoughts and feelings, and with the events which happen to us. As long as this is so, we are trapped in a shallow, highly personal life. But if we begin to listen to the voice of the real self, and come to accept it as the genuine heart of our life, we can reclaim our true heritage as a child of God. We can tap the power of *the impersonal life*.

Detaching from the mundane focus of the personal life and learning to identify with the voice of spirit is the theme of many, many books, but none describe this fundamental process of the spiritual path as clearly and comprehensively as *The Impersonal Life*. Written by Joseph S. Benner but published anonymously—to emphasize its basic message—*The Impersonal Life* is truly a classic statement of the power and nature of spirit.

In short, easy-to-read chapters, each written as a direct communication from the reader's own real self to his personality, *The Impersonal Life* describes the basic conflicts of human living, how they are resolved, and how resolving them advances the impersonal life of God.

There are also a number of excellent chapters which comment on a variety of overblown fictions of the "spiritual life," such as soul mates and spirit guides.

The Impersonal Life is a marvelous stimulus to personal and spiritual growth. It is highly recommended to all.

Narcissus & Goldmund
by Hermann Hesse

"The basic image in a good work of art is not a real, living figure, although it may inspire it. The basic image is not flesh and blood; it is mind. It is an image that has its home in the artist's soul."

Goldmund's words to his friend Narcissus touch the life force of this superb novel, quite possibly the greatest written by Hermann Hesse. For this is a story about human creativity—not in flesh and blood, but in the mind.

Narcissus is a medieval monk in a remote abbey. Goldmund comes to the abbey as a student. The two become friends, and Goldmund wants to be a monk like Narcissus. But Narcissus knows the cloistered life is not for his friend, and convinces him to find his life in the outer world. So Goldmund leaves to search for happiness in the world, first through romantic trysts with women, and then later as a sculptor. From time to time, his path takes him back to the abbey and Narcissus, but he never settles down. He continues to wander, searching for the vision which drives him onward—the vision which will fulfill his sense of being.

The friendship between Narcissus and Goldmund is strikingly similar to the ideal relationship between the soul and the personality. Each gives of his nature to the other and is enriched in return—and it is Narcissus who lives on, after his friend has died, to sustain the creative vision Goldmund has discovered.

Few stories are as powerful and as poignant as *Narcissus and Goldmund.*

Active Meditation
The Western Tradition
by Robert R. Leichtman, M.D. & Carl Japikse

There are two major elements in human consciousness: the personality, which we use in daily self-expression, and the higher self, which most of us largely ignore. The price we pay for ignoring the higher self, however, is an enormous one. It means we live without the enlightenment, love, and strength of our higher self.

Meditation is a set of practices which help us bring the life and power of the higher self into expression in the daily activities of the personality. The regular use of meditation enriches consciousness, illumines the mind, increases self-discipline, stimulates creativity, and integrates the personality with the higher self. It helps the personality attain the full potential of its design.

Effective meditation has been a part of every significant spiritual tradition in human history—because there is no better way of establishing contact between the personality and our higher self. There is no better way of tapping the divine energies of love, wisdom, and strength. There is no better path to enlightenment.

And yet, not all systems of meditation lead to enlightenment. In many systems, the art of meditation has been trivialized. Instead of serving as a method for establishing and maintaining contact with the higher self, it has all too often become a simple process of relaxing or quieting the mind and body—or concentrating on a single thought or sound. Many people accept these practices as legitimate aspects of meditation, but they are not.

Active Meditation: The Western Tradition, by Dr. Robert R. Leichtman and Carl Japikse, puts the art of meditation back in focus. Almost encyclopedic in scope, it is a comprehensive examination of the tradition, purpose, potential, and techniques of meditation. More importantly, it is a masterful statement of the emerging Western tradition of personal and spiritual growth. It is a book which challenges, inspires, enlightens, and informs. In fact, it sets the standard for meditation in the new age.

From beginning to end, the tone set by Leichtman and Japikse emphasizes the practical nature of meditation. To them, the subjects of meditation and personal growth are inseparable—the work of meditation should always be connected with the development of a greater capacity to act wisely and creatively in the physical plane. They decry the excessive passiveness which has crept into many systems of meditation, presenting instead a strong case that meditation is most effective when it is *active*. They state that the active practice of meditation *is* the Western tradition.

Active Meditation: The Western Tradition is therefore something more than just a precise definition of the art of meditation. It is also a thorough commentary on personal and spiritual growth. In specific, the authors describe:

- What meditation is—and is not.
- How meditation accelerates personal and spiritual growth.
- The nature of the higher self.
- How to contact the higher self.

- The proper relationship between the higher self and the personality.
- The work of integration.
- Skills of meditation and how to use them.
- Seven specific techniques of Active Meditation, for establishing an enlightened self-image, defining values and goals, mental housecleaning, healing the emotions, invoking wisdom, solving problems, and creative self-discovery.
- Meditating to help others.
- Group meditations.
- The evolution of consciousness.
- Problems associated with meditating and how to overcome them.

They also take on the task of exposing some of the more worn-out "sacred cows" of meditation and spiritual growth, which they handle very delightfully in a series of interludes with the angel "Herman." These slightly mischievous exchanges keep the book from getting too top heavy, as so many books on spiritual growth do, yet help us see the limits of many of the old traditions.

Throughout the book, Leichtman and Japikse work to strip away the vagueness and obscurity often associated with meditation and personal growth and treat their subject with common sense, clarity, and good humor. The result is a book which obviously does contain the seeds of a new tradition.

Active Meditation is a book which is easy to read and understand—yet also a book which will spur advanced meditators on to new discoveries, new realizations. It deserves to be the standard manual or reference book for all meditators.

The Bach Flower Remedies
by Edward Bach, M.D.

Dr. Edward Bach believed the heart of healing must be focused on the ills of the emotions—not physical distress. To him, the bodily ills are merely symptoms of far more serious problems—our fears, anxieties, apathy, depression, and hostility. In *The Bach Flower Remedies*, he sets forth his insights into health and illness—plus a remarkable system for treating the "ills of heart and spirit" with flower remedies.

The Bach Flower Remedies is actually three books in one. In the first section, "Heal Thyself," Dr. Bach discusses his spiritual perspective on the nature of illness and the ultimate source of effective cures to illness—the divinity within us. In specific, Dr. Bach says the human weaknesses that lead to illness need to be washed away by flooding our consciousness with a strong dose of the spiritual qualities that will neutralize them. To aid in this process, Dr. Bach recommends the use of flower remedies—the essences of flowers which, when taken in the form of elixirs, act as antidotes to the emotional poisons which lead to illness.

The use of these remedies is described in the book's second section, "The Twelve Healers." The final section, "The Bach Remedies Repertory" by F.J. Wheeler, M.D., is a detailed account of the value of each of the 38 flower remedies and how to use them.

Just reading this book is a health-giving experience. But its real power lies in using the remedies to bring us into harmony with the God within us—and the divine power of Love.

The Tao of Meow
by Waldo Japussy

New translations of Lao Tzu's classic commentary on power and spirit, *The Tao Te Ching*, have always been eagerly accepted by the reading public. There is something timeless and profound about these 81 verses by the ancient Chinese philosopher.

The Tao of Meow is not just another translation of this ancient classic, however. It is an original philosophic statement by Waldo Japussy, the eldest cat in the household of Rose and Carl Japikse. The Japikses always suspected that Waldo was a superior cat, ever since he first came into their lives. But it was only when Carl was about to throw away a sheaf of papers that had been "ruined" by Waldo walking across them with dirty paws—and he suddenly realized that the paw prints formed a coherent pattern of poetic stanzas—that they began to understand Waldo's true mission here on earth. Carl sat down immediately to try to make sense of Waldo's "writings." Months later, he realized that the text he had mistaken for muddy paw prints was actually a sophisticated restatement of Lao Tzu's ancient verses—from a cat's purrspective.

In this new translation, Waldo reveals that the true name of the Tao is "Meow," which will come as no surprise to cat lovers. Before Heaven and Earth were formed, the Meow existed. It is the essence of life within all living things. In humans, as Waldo explains it, it is virtue that reveals the presence of the Meow. In cats, it is the mystical ability to walk through an unmown field and not get any burrs in their coat of fur. Through the correct use of the Meow, Waldo is able to get his way. And while that may not be exactly what Lao Tzu had in mind, it is certainly all that Waldo wants.

The spirit of *The Tao of Meow* is best captured by this excerpt:

> Humans have a mind, but never use it;
> The Wise Cat learns to use it for them.
> The Tao of Meow is the highest form of
>   simplicity—
> If you do the thinking for humans,
> They will do your work for you.
> They will even tell all their friends
>   how you have outwitted them,
> And everyone will agree that you are "cute."

The text is illustrated by reproductions of the original paw print manuscript as written by Waldo.

The Tao of Meow is a witty, wise, and wonderful book that will make you purr.

War in Heaven
by Charles Williams

The place is England; the time is the 1930's. A number of different factions—an Anglican priest, a Catholic duke, the bewildered employees of a publishing house, a nasty crowd of satanists, and a powerful mage who is the magical "protector" of the graal—are vying with one another in search of the holy graal, the cup which Jesus used at the Last Supper.

The graal means something quite different to each group. It is a doorway to power for the satanists, a historical oddity to the publishers, an immensely significant relic to the duke, a point where the love of God can be experienced to the priest, and a visible symbol of the presence of God on earth to its protector.

Against a thrilling plot of supernatural mystery and murder, Williams weaves a masterful theme: that the real graal is the soul—the true vessel of spirit within us—and the ultimate prize of our spiritual search is its power, love, and wisdom. In the novel, the graal is first stolen, then attacked psychically, and finally almost destroyed. Simultaneously, the lives and sanity of many of the major characters undergo similar perils. In the end, however, divine powers triumph and evil is defeated by the courageous acts of a few of the characters.

The real war in heaven is the struggle within us between the elements of our personal weakness and our spiritual strength. Charles Williams has written a powerful novel which should be read by all students of the mysteries of the spiritual path.

Myth Conceptions
by Robert Asprin

A demon who has lost his powers, Aahz still manages to keep his apprentice, Skeeve, out of most kinds of trouble. Then Skeeve is summoned to audition for the post of Court Magician. Unfortunately, he gets the job.

How can Aahz and Skeeve defend the kingdom against the mightiest army in the world? If they win, they will be executed—if they lose, they will be killed. What kind of magic can beat these odds? A rare kind of magic, indeed—the magic of author Robert Asprin, who combines a rollicking good sense of humor with high fantasy to shape a story that reminds us that life is filled with things that are not what they seem to be. We need the good sense to laugh at life and see it for what it really is.

Myth Conceptions is packed with fast-paced adventures revolving around Aahz, Skeeve, a king who tries not to reign, and an army which is actually fighting only so it can pay off its bar and gambling bills. In each case, the public image or myth of each character differs vastly from his or her private nature. At times, this embarrasses them—but at other times the myth saves them from disaster, as it affects the way everyone else treats them.

Myth Conceptions reminds us that there are often contradictions between what we seem to be and who we actually are. Sometimes we stumble over the myth; sometimes we live up to it; but in either case, our personal myth helps us stretch our character.

This is a book no one should myth.

Health and Light
by John N. Ott

The importance of light to human consciousness and health has long been known esoterically. Now its value is being proven scientifically, through the pioneer work of John N. Ott.

John Ott is the developer of time-lapse photography. He became famous for the sequences he filmed for the movie, *On A Clear Day You Can See Forever*. While working with time-lapse photography of flowers, Ott noticed certain flowers did not grow well under artificial lighting, indoors. He began to suspect that these flowers—and humans beings, too—need the full spectrum of light which comes from the sun, not just the narrow bands of light which enable us to see.

He proceeded to conduct a series of experiments which have confirmed his suspicions—and taught him a great deal more about the nature of light as well. He has discovered, for example, that tinted eyeglasses can increase emotional reactiveness, that television radiation can induce fatigue and hyperkinesis in children, that the proper use of light can help treat cancer, and that arthritis is aggravated by improper light conditions.

Ott's findings are set forth in *Health and Light*, the story of his observations, experiments and discoveries. It is also the story of the true scientific method at work—and how seldom those who control scientific research appreciate and support genuine creative efforts.

Health and Light is highly recommended for the new light it sheds on light itself.

The New View Over Atlantis
by John Michell

In 1921, the British merchant Alfred Watkins had a psychic vision which propelled him centuries into the past and revealed to him a precise network of straight lines crisscrossing the English countryside in a geometric pattern. Watkins realized that churches, monuments, roads, and earthworks had all been built on these lines, as though there were a purpose linking them all in some mysterious way. He came to call these channels "ley lines."

Watkin's announcement of ley lines led to a renewed interest in the significance of geomantic design. Eight years later, for example, Kathryn Maltwood found that the landscape about Glastonbury Cathedral was filled with mounds and natural folds representing the signs of the zodiac. Other keen observers made similar discoveries as well, finding that the ancient Druids had used hills, springs, plains, and rivers to form temples several miles in length.

But brilliant and important discoveries often fade into the background after an initial flurry of interest—and this seemed to be the fate of these discoveries until the publication in 1969 of *The View Over Atlantis* by John Michell. Michell had researched the work of Watkins, Maltwood, and others, updated it, and retold it in an absorbing and stimulating book.

Now, Michell has updated his own work and issued *The **New** View Over Atlantis*, with a great deal of additional material. Like the earlier book, this one gives a full account of ley lines, and then goes on to present a new commentary on the mystical significance of numbers in ancient architecture and city planning.

Underlying it all is the very strong thesis that the ley lines are to the earth what acupuncture meridians are to the etheric body of the human being. Michell presents striking evidence that the planet earth is not just an inert ball of dirt and rock, but actually *a living body of giant intelligence with arteries of living energy that circulates throughout the surface of the earth.* The ancients, he suggests, knew of this living nature of physical energy and took it into account as they planned their cities, temples, and landscaping.

One of the most fascinating aspects of this book is the deft way in which Michell documents knowledge of ley lines in all cultures throughout the world. In one chapter, for instance, he delves into Chinese myths and geomancy. According to Michell, there is a strong tradition in China for facilitating the unimpeded flow of the earth's vital energy by moving hills and redirecting streams. The Chinese are also careful to locate shrines, burial sites, and homes in conjunction with these lines.

Michell also brilliantly relates the mythological symbolism of the dragon in China with similar myths in English folklore. The Chinese dragon is actually an aspect of the earth's vitality. It flows along the ley lines, bringing an extra charge of energy to the land. In early English myths, the dragon is much the same— a great benevolent power that is a source of natural vitality when properly tamed and focused. The idea that the dragon is an evil force apparently arose only after the Church became threatened by these pagan tales and sought ways to discredit them.

The second half of the book, in which Michell discusses the mystical value of numbers, is equally fascinating. Ancient sacred buildings, he found, were built not only at the crossing of two or more ley lines, but also in accord with mystical symbolism and the structure of numbers. Number was held by the ancients to be the first archetype of nature, with everything in creation eventually conforming to this order in terms of its shapes, patterns, and cycles.

This is a remarkable book, not just for the information it imparts but also for the way it stimulates the thinking mind. Colin Wilson, the author of *The Mind Parasites*, hailed *The New View Over Atlantis* as "one of the great seminal books of our generation."

Michell himself makes the point that "revelation comes to those who invoke it through intense studies and a lively curiosity of mind." *The New View Over Atlantis* stands as a lucid revelation of the relationship between myth and civilization, alchemy and science, and astronomy and acupuncture.

As Michell writes, "No form of study can be more delightful and beneficial than this one, for in pondering the designs and works of the ancient sages one is exposed to the noblest mentalities of our kind, which these works reflect." For this reason alone, *The New View Over Atlantis* is a book to be read by every thinking person.

A Whack on the Side of the Head

by Roger von Oech

We're all ... [illegible] into neat pigeon-holes — or not. And really, we tend to cling to high ideals and narrow prospects ... [illegible] word ... [illegible]situations ... [illegible] it. both of ... [illegible]

A Whack on the Side of the Head
by Roger von Oech

We are all far more creative than most of us realize—or admit. As a result, we tend to cling to highly personal, narrow perspectives of life—in work, our relationships, and our beliefs. These narrow perspectives often cause us to miss creative opportunities, as well as invitations from the higher self to enrich our self-understanding and grow as a human being.

Perhaps we get fired from our job. We digest this event in our traditional, narrow perspective and decide that we have been a failure. Our self-esteem plunges. We become depressed. We wonder bitterly how such a terrible thing could happen to such a nice person. The higher self, however, may have an entirely different perspective. It may have seen how our present job has caused us to stagnate and fail to develop our potential. But because we are unwilling to leave the security of our job, it must arrange to have us dismissed, so that we can go on to the next phase of our career. Six months from now, when we are comfortably settled in our new position, we may be able to see this larger perspective, too. But right now, we are stuck in a narrow, blind view of life and current events.

What we need, according to Roger von Oech, is a whack on the side of the head. And that is what the higher self delivers.

Von Oech has been teaching creative and innovative thinking for a number of years, primarily among the nation's work force. He has found that the vast majority of people he teaches are stuck in one-dimensional, narrow perspectives. And this makes it very difficult for them to learn to think creatively—until they loosen up and start looking at life in new ways.

This is the purpose of his excellent book, *A Whack on the Side of the Head*—to inspire us to look at life in new ways and turn on our capacity for creative and innovative thinking. He does this by challenging our assumptions and normal ways of processing facts and data.

For example, he might ask the seemingly silly question, "What do cats and refrigerators have in common?" The average person would answer, "Nothing." A cat lover might reply, "You can always find a cat next to the refrigerator." But once you let yourself be whacked on the side of the head, you can start to see all kinds of similarities. They both have tails. They both purr. They both swallow fish. And so on.

In chapter after chapter, von Oech uses this kind of half-serious approach to get us to develop alternative methods to solve life's problems. The book is chock full of useful means to break down our thought barriers and learn to use the ideas that come to us.

In addition, von Oech has developed what he calls the "Creative Whack Pack," a deck of 64 cards which can be used like the I Ching to stimulate creative ideas. While not as profound as the I Ching, the Whack Pack nonetheless can be very helpful in triggering new awareness of how to act in solving problems.

Both the book and Whack Pack are highly recommended, not only for people who are already creative but also for the many others who need a good whack on the side of the head.

Glory Road
by Robert Heinlein

"There are things which cannot be taught in ten easy lessons, nor popularized for the masses; they take years of sweat. This be treason in an age when ignorance has come into its own and one man's opinion is as good as another's. But there it is."

Treason, of course, is just a "t" beyond "reason." And, in the marvelous fantasy world of Robert Heinlein, treason to three-car garages, cocktail parties, and similar cultural "necessities" leads us out of the kingdom of ignorance and onto the glory road. The glory road, in this particular case, begins on a beach of the French Riviera and ends at the center of the cosmos. Scar, a young American, is asked by Star, the empress of 20 universes, to help her retrieve the Egg of the Phoenix, which contains the knowledge of all her predecessors, from Soul-Eater, who stole it from her.

Before the egg is regained, it becomes clear that the betrayal of ignorance and materialism is anything but treason. It is the stuff of which true heroes—and the spiritual life—are made. For the glory road is really the spiritual path. To travel it, one must be ready to leave behind the roads the average person chooses to follow. He must embrace the magic of the soul and marry himself to its strength. And he must defeat the obstacles which would knock him off the path.

Glory Road is as much an adventure into our own assumptions, beliefs, and heroism as it is a story of Scar and Star. For anyone who likes fantasy, this is a glorious novel.

Across the Unknown
by Stewart Edward White

Before he began writing books based on the psychic explorations of his wife Betty, Stewart Edward White was already a well-established writer of adventure stories—stories of the wild west, untamed Africa, and frigid Alaska. So it was only natural for White to consider the psychic investigations of his wife one more kind of adventure in uncharted regions.

Indeed, *Across the Unknown* is much more than testimony that such dimensions do exist. It is a comprehensive effort to map these inner regions of consciousness and make the unknown known. But White is not satisfied with giving us only a vicarious tour of the invisible levels of life. He insists on showing us how to make the journey on our own, so that we are not dependent on anyone else's testimony.

The result is a practical, easy-to-read, and entertaining description of what it means to refine our awareness and nurture the ability to operate consciously at all levels of our being, the intuitive as well as the physical. As White puts it, *Across the Unknown* is "a formula for living." It reveals how the inner dimensions are alive in each of us, even while immersed in the physical plane. And it shows us how to tap the reality of the unknown to enrich our life.

Across the Unknown is one of the most important books ever written about the inner planes. As Betty says, "It is essential to linger frequently on the frontier of one's limitations, looking out eagerly across the unknown." This book helps us do just that.

Initiation
by Elisabeth Haich

"The higher self—God—always finds a human mouth when he has a message for us. For the self there is no such thing as an obstacle."

There is no such thing as an obstacle. This quiet phrase, in a chapter near the conclusion of this epic novel, nicely sums up the spirit that pervades the whole of the book. *Initiation* is a story of great internal struggle and conflict—a story of failure to seize the opportunity of initiation. And yet, even failure of this magnitude is not a disgrace, but the basis for triumph. In this dramatic way, we vividly learn that there is no obstacle which can defeat the soul.

This is an autobiographical novel, set both at the time of the second world war and in ancient Egypt. It is the story of a twentieth-century aspirant who does not fully understand the powerful struggle of her life, until she psychically remembers her training for initiation in the mystery temples of Egypt, the trials of the initiation itself, and the unredeemed weakness which leads her to fail the test.

But she does not really fail. The test merely continues on and is resumed, after a series of lives, in this century, against the backdrop of war. In this way, we are subtly reminded that the tests of the individual transpire in the context of the tests of humanity. The initiation of the individual makes sense only in the context of the initiation of humanity.

There is a great measure of wisdom in *Initiation*. It, too, has a message from the higher self to us.

The Fountainhead
by Ayn Rand

Ayn Rand writes novels which are set in "the way things are," but move us toward a deeper, more profound realization of "the way things ought to be."

In *The Fountainhead*, Miss Rand tells the story of Howard Roark, an architect who refuses to surrender either his individuality or creative integrity. He thereby incurs the wrath and opposition of most of the rest of the characters—petty people who neither appreciate nor understand his genius. They are attracted to Roark by the thought of benefiting from his talent. But when they find they cannot profit from it, they turn on him and try to destroy him.

To Ayn Rand, Howard Roark sums up the ideals of self-actualization and creative genius. He is a man who has tapped the "fountainhead" of inspiration and brilliance within himself, and is guided by it, in spite of the bitter opposition he encounters. He is a man about whom Miss Rand can write, quoting Nietzsche, "The noble soul has reverence for itself."

It is rare to find an author who recognizes the inherent nobility of human life and presents it in its proper light, not romanticizing it but forcefully dramatizing its strength, value, purpose, and reality. It is likewise rare to find a novel which so continually prods us to *think* and reevaluate our idea of what counts in life.

The Fountainhead is a classic of modern American literature. It deserves to be—and it deserves to be read by everyone striving to fulfill the promise of human nobility and genius.

The Mind Parasites
by Colin Wilson

Surely one of the most important pieces of fiction to emerge so far in this century is *The Mind Parasites*, a novel by Colin Wilson. First published in 1967, it is a powerful story about the reactiveness found in the collective subconscious of humanity, how it influences the average person, and how it can be overcome.

In brief, *The Mind Parasites* is a science fiction tale about the archeologist Gilbert Austin and his confrontation with the Tsathogguans, denizens of the mental deep who in effect attempt to take control of human civilization. They endeavor to destroy Austin and his colleagues, but as Austin discovers their true nature, he grows in his understanding and capacity to destroy them.

Ultimately, the action leads to global warfare, the psychokinetic movement of the moon, and final victory in outer space. Yet for all these exciting and suspenseful adventures, the real story of *The Mind Parasites* transpires at a deeper, more profound dimension—in the collective subconscious of the human race.

There *is* a collective subconscious for the whole race, and it is just as real and active as our own personal subconsciouses. It is filled with the collective fears, animosities, laziness, and parasitism of the human race—and has been building in force and scope since the beginning of mankind.

In no way is this collective subconscious to be confused with the noble and divine spirit which all humanity share; that would more appropriately be called the "supraconscious." The collective subconscious, by contrast, is entirely of mankind's own making. While some of the elements within it are good and partly enlightened, many of them are not. The collective subconscious has very strong attitudes about what is right and proper and works hard to preserve the status quo. It enshrines pettiness, the lowest common denominator, and mob attitudes, such as violence.

One of the repeated themes in *The Mind Parasites* is that this collective subconscious will fight any radical departure from the norms of society, including genius. Indeed, the novel begins with the suicide of a close friend of Austin's—a man of brilliance who learned too much about the nature of the mind parasites and thus became a threat. In retaliation, the parasites drove him to suicide.

To some who read this book, it may seem to be a novel of paranoia, but it most assuredly is not. It is a brilliant description of the psychic reality of the collective subconscious and its persistent resistance to new ideas, genius, and individuality. Time and again, it drives home the message that mass consciousness will attack and try to destroy men and women of genius. It is sad but true that people of genius appear and thrive *in spite of* mass consciousness.

In many ways, *The Mind Parasites* is virtually a textbook on how to neutralize the influence of mass consciousness. As Austin meets challenge after challenge, he discovers the absolute necessity of focusing the personal will to overcome his own self-doubt and the intrusion of alien ideas into his thinking.

But even that, he finds, is limited in its value.

He learns that this personal will must be used in a larger perspective, not as an expression of one's selfishness. And the power of the personal will is not just something to *believe* in; it must be dynamically expressed as well.

Ultimately, he learns that it is the overshadowing power of divine love, blended with the will, which is most effective in meeting the resistance of the mind parasites. From that point on, Austin is clearly in charge of the situation; we do not doubt that he will triumph, but there are still a number of surprises involved in just how he manages to do it.

This is a novel of tremendous insight—a story which totally captivates the imagination of the perceptive reader. Once begun, it is nearly impossible to set down; once finished, it is put away reluctantly, with the wish that it were longer. This wish is mitigated, however, by the realization that here is a book worth rereading several times.

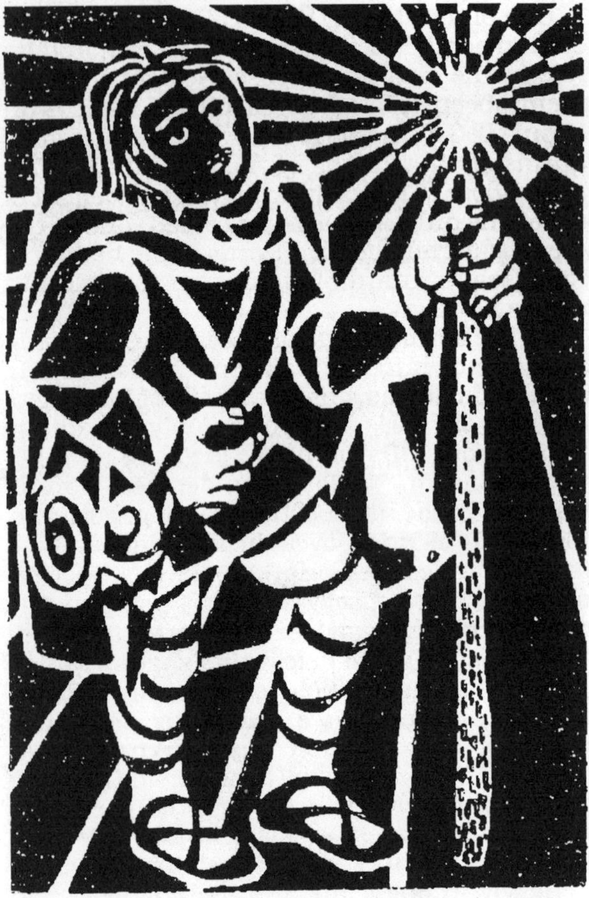

The Earthsea Trilogy
by Ursula LeGuin

One of the classic themes of literature is the eternal conflict between good and evil, and its role in the creative process. Seldom has this theme been treated as effectively as it is in Ursula LeGuin's trilogy of novels: *The Wizard of Earthsea*, *The Tombs of Atuan*, and *The Farthest Shore*. This exciting and fast-paced set of novels records the Odyssey of Ged, one of the greatest archmages or wizards in the history of Earthsea, a group of islands on a world not unlike our own.

As *The Wizard of Earthsea* begins, Ged is only a boy, known to most as "Sparrowhawk." He soon finds he has a natural instinct for magic. At first, he uses his power only to amuse himself, but after he uses his gift to save his village from an invasion, he undergoes rigorous training. In the midst of this training, however, his youthful pride overwhelms him, and he foolishly unleashes a dark, malevolent power, almost killing himself. From that point on, the dark force he has unloosed begins to stalk Ged.

Ged's struggle to defeat this shadow which pursues him is symbolic of the many difficulties we all face as we travel our path—our Odyssey—and confront our weaknesses. At first, Ged believes the evil to be outside himself, an ancient power which reentered the world during his moment of magical folly. He sees himself as the hunted, and despairs of escape.

Slowly, though, his attitude changes, and Ged becomes the hunter, not the hunted. He chases the dark force about the world, finally engaging it in a battle to the death at the edge of the earth. Only then, in this extreme state, does Ged realize he cannot escape it, for it is *within.* He is dealing with his own dark nature. This recognition enables him to triumph.

In *The Tombs of Atuan*, the narrative shifts to the training of Arha, the priestess of the Tombs, the Domain of the Nameless Ones, the gods of an ancient religion. As priestess, Arha must guard the Tombs and their large underground labyrinth, which is the repository of much power and ancient treasures. The life of Arha is quiet and undisturbed, until Ged arrives as a thief in the night, to search the tombs for a ring which long ago was the property of Erreth-Akbe, the most powerful magician Earthsea had ever known. When almost defeated by evil, Erreth-Akbe broke the ring and hid the two parts. Ever since, Earthsea has not been at peace.

Having found one half of the ring, Ged is searching for the other half. Arha discovers Ged and decides to destroy him, but finds herself strangely reluctant to do so. Eventually, Ged convinces Arha that she guards the powers of darkness, not the powers of light.

Ged finds the second half of the ring and unites the two, but he is still controlled by Arha, just as the far more powerful and wise force of our spirit often becomes trapped by the doubting, materialistic grip of the earthbound personality dominated by superstition, tradition, fear, and ritual. Working only with his wisdom, love, and faith, Ged does eventually conquer Arha's mind and will, leading her to forsake her underground labyrinths and religious dogma and embrace her true individuality.

In the third novel, *The Farthest Shore*, Ged has become the archmage of Earthsea, the most powerful of all wizards. As such, he must confront a problem afflicting the whole of civilization: the magical power of Earthsea is quickly fading. Since magic is essential to almost everything in Earthsea, even manufacture, the failure of magic is a dire threat.

After many adventures, Ged discovers that the cause of this problem is a selfish magician who has sought to attain physical immortality by sucking the life out of everything around him. To confront him, Ged travels first to the farthest shore of Earthsea, and then to an even farther shore, passing into the land of the dead. With the help of dragons, Ged destroys his opponent and closes the door between the forces of darkness and light, before returning to his own body.

Through this story of battle between one who *serves* the divine plan and one who is selfish at the expense of everyone else, we are given a rich and symbolic description of the conflicts which plague our own civilization.

Indeed, these three stories are much, much more than just enchanting tales. They translate the everyday struggles of the spiritual aspirant to mythical proportions, giving us a framework in which to view our own problems more intelligently. They also help us see the power of the magic in our lives—the magic of spirit.

The Earthsea Trilogy is a work of magic itself.

There is a River
by Thomas Sugrue

It has now been almost fifty years since the death of Edgar Cayce. At that time, his work as a psychic was little known. Now, thanks to a number of popular biographies and countless books on his readings, Edgar Cayce has become the best-known psychic in America. When people first start reading about the inner life and spiritual growth, it is almost surely a book about Cayce that they begin with.

Yet with all the profusion of books about Cayce and his work, the very first one ever written, Thomas Sugrue's *There is a River*, remains by far the best biography and introduction to Cayce's philosophy and readings. In all likelihood, this is because it is written by a professional author who knew Cayce as a friend, and was able to draw on first-hand research, not just the myths and interpretations which have arisen over the years since Cayce died.

And the story of *There is a River* is a fascinating one. Cayce richly deserves the fame which has come to him; during his life, he gave more than 15,000 readings in which he diagnosed physical problems and suggested cures, reported on previous lives and karmic residue, advised on spiritual growth, and even gave suggestions for business and creative projects. He also had the foresight to have these trances stenographically recorded, so the transcripts would be available for further research. It is this treasure that makes his work so valuable.

There is a River is a marvelous introduction to the life and work of an important psychic.

Healing & Regeneration Through Color & Music
by Corinne Heline

The many colors of light, as well as the many tones of music, are wavelengths of living energy. We are affected by the colors and music of our environment and—if we understand the esoteric principles of energy—we can harness both color and music to heal ourselves and others, mentally, emotionally, and physically.

Corinne Heline studied the impact of the energies of color and music throughout her long career in new age work, and wrote two classics on the subject, *Healing and Regeneration Through Color* and *Healing and Regeneration Through Music*. These two books have now been combined in a single volume.

In her essay on color, Mrs. Heline explores the esoteric principles of color, its supernatural powers, its relationship to music, and how it can be used both for healing physical ailments and building solid character values. In the treatise on music, she expands on the same themes, but applies them to the principle of harmony and musical tones. She also explores the deeper significances of great music.

These two essays are especially powerful because of the many practical suggestions Mrs. Heline makes for the use of both color and music. She packs a tremendous amount of information into a relatively short space—information that each reader will be able to readily use for healing and regeneration.

This is a first-rate source of insight.

A Soul's Journey
by Peter Richelieu

Out-of-body travel has long been a fascinating topic for occult writers, but most books on the subject have been nothing more than travelogues exploring the author's own rich fantasies. Peter Richelieu's *A Soul's Journey*, however, offers a great deal more than the standard fare. It is a first-hand account of travel in the various levels of the astral and mental planes.

The book is written in narrative style, recounting the journeys of Henry, an Englishman living in Ceylon at the time of the second world war. The account begins with Henry grieving over the death of his brother Charles, a British soldier. His grief invokes the appearance of Acharya, a holy man from India, who lectures him about the phenomena of the inner life and events after death.

But Acharya's instruction does not stop there. Using special techniques, he enables Henry to leave his body during the hours of sleep so that he can be taken on a guided tour of the inner, subtle planes of creation. Each night, Henry takes a powerful drug to ensure sleep and travels in his subtle bodies through many adventures on the subplanes of the astral and mental levels.

First, Acharya leads Henry to visit his brother Charles, to see that he has not actually "died." After that, Henry is taught much about the rich opportunities of the inner planes for education and growth—both for the so-called "dead" and for people who can visit the inner planes while asleep.

It is rare to find a book which gives any description of the inner planes except those levels closest to the physical. It should be understood that this book is not just an account of the pretty scenery we might encounter at low psychic levels. Instead, Richelieu provides us with a clear account of the hospitals and colleges of the inner planes, the great halls of knowledge and wisdom. In addition, there are interesting reports of how spirits visit the physical plane and mingle among us, usually without our awareness.

Henry learns about the training given to people when they first arrive on the inner planes after death and observes several occult and religious ceremonies first-hand. Eventually, he is taken by Acharya to the mental plane. It is likely that this is the only book in print, outside the writings of C.W. Leadbeater, which gives an accurate account of the uncanny experiences of dealing directly with the force of ideas, communicating telepathically, and being totally free of cloying emotions.

The use of a drug to visit the inner planes may be a bit of fiction, as it would not be a standard spiritual practice. But this is not a book on how to leave the body and travel on the inner planes. It is a rare and unusually precise account of the nature and activities of the inner life.

Far from describing the heaven worlds as places of "rest" and "peace," which is silly, *A Soul's Journey* leads us into a realm of tremendous activity, healing, and teaching. The book emphasizes the fact that we all have a rich life on the inner planes, whether or not we can visit them consciously, as a result of having finer bodies made of the subtle matter of these inner realms. Thus, it is possible to be taught and healed on these inner levels, even while still in the physical body. Richelieu opens to us many new possibilities for extending the range of our education and experience—while our physical body sleeps.

One of the most important messages for all of us to learn is that we have an existence on the inner side of life *right now*, not just after we die. We are all endowed with the potential to tap the higher dimensions of life, even while in the physical.

Reading *A Soul's Journey* helps give us fresh insight into this dynamic principle. Even though most of us are not likely to have vivid conscious memories of what transpires on the inner planes while we are asleep, as Henry did, we do tend to bring through the wisdom we gain into our waking hours, as nudges, insights, and new awareness. It is valuable to learn as much about this process as possible. Richelieu also leaves us with much to ponder on regarding the influences of the higher dimensions on our activities here in the physical plane.

In fact, *A Soul's Journey* is really everyone's odyssey.

(Originally published as **From The Turret)**

Prodigal Genius
by John J. O'Neill

Nikola Tesla spent his lifetime making the impossible possible—and doing it with brilliance, style, and seeming ease. He made practical the generation of alternating current, which electrical scientists had thought impossible. He developed a system for long distance transmission of electricity, which Thomas Edison had thought impossible. He broadcast electricity through the air without wires, which many experts *still* think impossible. He was truly a prodigal genius.

Prodigal Genius is the story of Nikola Tesla's life and work. It is not just a biography of Tesla, however. It is also one of the most remarkable explorations of human genius and creativity in print. For within the story of Tesla's life there is another story as well—the story of an enlightened and noble mind at work, examining the archetypal laws and patterns of the universe and doing something with them!

There are important lessons in this book for every reader—lessons about creativity, the enlightened use of energy, the psychic aspects of genius, and the public tendency to ignore its great geniuses. Some of the lessons lie between the lines, but the story is so skillfully told that we are inspired to look for them—and learn.

While many biographies have now been written about Tesla, John O'Neill's still stands as the most insightful. O'Neill knew Tesla personally, and was a Pulitzer Prize-winning author of scientific writings.

Like Tesla himself, this biography *glows*.

The Secret Teachings of All Ages
by Manly P. Hall

Manly P. Hall is one of this century's most important chroniclers of the mysteries of the spiritual life, and *The Secret Teachings of All Ages* is unquestionably the keystone of his writings, a rich and marvelous treasure of esoteric knowledge.

Amply illustrated and handsomely printed, *The Secret Teachings of All Ages* is a compendium of occult lore—and a delight to read. There is an incredible wealth of information in this volume, covering every major area of the mysteries:

- Atlantis.
- The Egyptian & Greek mysteries.
- Astrology.
- The Qabalah.
- The Tarot.
- Alchemy.
- The science of numbers.
- The esoteric roots of freemasonry.
- The esoteric message of world religions.

This is not a book that espouses a limited doctrine; it is broad and expansive, embracing all of the major esoteric and spiritual traditions and demonstrating the contributions each has made to world thought and understanding. As such, it is a book that can help acquaint us with the tremendous depth of human knowledge.

The Secret Teachings of All Ages is an encyclopedic book that belongs in the library of everyone seriously interested in the mysteries.

The Ancient of Days

A**hole No More!
by Dr. Xavier Crement

One of the great problems afflicting modern humanity is the large number of people addicted to assholism. Until now, there has been no authoritative statement on this disease; it has been one of those subjects that everyone knows about but no one has the courage to discuss.

Dr. Crement, who began his career in proctology but has since switched to psychiatry, corrects this glaring omission with this encyclopedic treatment of assholism. The book is written primarily as a self-help guide for recovering assholes—people who have come to grips with their addiction and are trying to learn what it means to be a decent human being. But it also includes a thorough description of the causes of assholism, the presence of assholism in business, government, education, religion, and the media, and the terrible waste of man hours and creativity to this menace.

There are also special sections dealing with:
- Adult children of asshole parents.
- Married to an asshole.
- When your best friend is an asshole.
- Massholism.
- Morassholism—bureaucratic assholism.
- When society becomes an asshole.
- The 12 steps to recovering from assholism.

This is a hilarious book—one of the best spoofs ever written. But it is actually more than just a humor book, for underneath the jokes there is an unusual amount of truth. It reminds us of what it means to be a decent human being.

The Practice of the Presence of God
by Brother Lawrence

Brother Lawrence was a Carmelite friar who lived 350 years ago. It was not what he did that made him famous, nor even what he wrote. Before he became a monk, he was a soldier and courtier; as a monk, he worked primarily in the kitchen and the shoe shop. And he destroyed almost everything he wrote, thinking it was unworthy. This small book is a collection of the few letters and reflections that survived.

No, the reason why Brother Lawrence is remembered is because of the *way* he lived his life—in specific, the grace and devotion he exuded even as he pursued his commonplace, menial chores.

Brother Lawrence is a wonderful model of the God-filled life, and these writings provide marvelous insights into just what it means—not in theory, but in deeds—to practice the presence of God. Each day, Brother Lawrence endeavored to do just that—to make sure that his thoughts and acts were centered in a constant communion with God.

It was his own superior, Abbé Joseph de Beaufort, who was so inspired by the example of this monk that he collected these remaining writings after Brother Lawrence died and had them published.

The Practice of the Presence of God is as fresh and relevant to our lives today as when it was written. It challenges each of us to likewise practice the presence of God in all that we do.

Siddhartha

by Hermann Hesse

Siddhartha is a Brahmin youth in India who seeks the spiritual path. He therefore leaves his father's house to become a traveling ascetic, taking with him his childhood friend, Govinda.

Siddhartha is an exceptionally gifted ascetic, able to withstand the deprivations of self-denial with little trouble. But he does not find enlightenment through the life of asceticism. As he tells Govinda, "What I have so far learned from the Samanas, I could have learned more quickly and easily in every inn in a prostitute's quarters." So he leaves the ranks of the ascetics, and travels to hear the Buddha. From listening to the Buddha, he realizes what he has been searching for: knowledge of himself. But he also realizes that no teacher, even the Buddha, can give him that knowledge.

Govinda becomes a disciple of the Buddha, but Siddhartha plunges into the swirl of human activity, taking on a lover and becoming a merchant. He grows rich, but gradually realizes he is a stranger in the world of the average man. His real interest lies in discovering who he is.

At the peak of his success, he walks away from it and settles by a river. It is just an ordinary river, but to Siddhartha, it becomes the river of life. He studies its rhythms and harmonies and, by learning what the river is, he also learns who he is. And once he has learned, finally, what he has sought after so diligently, his friend Govinda comes to him again, and Siddhartha shares what he has learned.

Siddhartha is an eloquent, moving story.

Saga of the Well World
by Jack L. Chalker

"I want to die, boy. I want to die—and I can't. Not ever. Not at all. And I want death so very much."

Varnett shook his head uncomprehendingly. "I can't figure you, Brazil. I just can't figure you."

"What do you want, Varnett?" Brazil asked, changing tone. "What would you wish for yourself?"

I've thought a lot about that," the other replied. "I'm only 15 years old, Brazil. Just 15. My world has always been dehumanized people and cold mathematics. I'm the oldest 15 of my race, now, though. I think, perhaps, I'd like to enjoy life, enjoy a human life—and somehow make my contribution to progress. To stop this headlong rush of the human race into a Markovian hell and try to build the society they hoped would evolve from their tens of thousands of cultures and races. There's a greatness here in the Markovian Well, a potential unrealized, but great nonetheless. I'd like to see it reached, to complete the equations the Markovians couldn't."

"So would I, boy," Brazil replied earnestly. "For then I could die."

In this scrap of dialogue between one of the youngest products of creation and one of the oldest, Jack L. Chalker encapsulates the hope of the universe he has so brilliantly created in his five-novel series, *Saga of the Well World*. Nathan Brazil cannot die because it is his destiny to preserve the universe from destruction. He has lived since the beginning of the Markovian universe, and cannot die until the drama of creation is completed. And there are all kinds of cunning, devious, and selfish people, races, and societies who are all too willing to risk destroying the whole universe in order to seize control of it.

Brazil, the prototypal "wandering Jew," moves in and out of the lives of these people and societies, not always remembering who he is or what he has done in the past, but remaining a servant of the creative ideals it is his duty to protect. When we first meet Brazil, he is captain of a space freighter. But as the story of the first book, *Midnight at the Well of Souls*, unfolds, Brazil is drawn to the Well World, where a magnificent civilization once flourished and then disappeared.

The people of this ancient civilization were the Markovians, masters of the secrets of creation—including the ability to generate new forms of life and to change existing forms into totally different ones—changing, for example, a human being into a 500-pound creature who is a walrus at the upper end and a snake at the lower. Actually, Markovian science is not dead at all—it turns out to be quite active. And as this news spreads throughout the universe, the Well World, with its Well of Souls, becomes the object of war, greed, and selfishness.

The remaining four novels in the epic series—*Exile at the Well of Souls, Quest for the Well of Souls, The Return of Nathan Brazil,* and *Twilight at the Well of Souls*—chronicle these conflicts and struggles, and the central role played by Brazil in keeping life in the universe evolving as it is meant to. Indeed, it slowly becomes apparent that Brazil is not acting on his own, but as an agent of universal intelligence and order, a central feature of Markovian science. The development of new life forms, the transfer of consciousness from one form to another, and the struggle between good and evil are all regulated in an orderly fashion.

As in real life, the rules and destiny which govern these events have been laid out by divine intelligence, but the characters are allowed to stumble through their paces on their own. The outcome is not guaranteed, even though the principles of evolution are.

In this way, Chalker takes a fascinating story, endows it with a complex plot, striking characters, and surprising twists, and then uses it to convey a number of esoteric themes of importance: reincarnation, the evolution of consciousness, good versus evil, and the dualities of the personality and the soul, consciousness and matter. In general, Chalker is able to communicate these ideas more effectively in these novels than other writers have been able to in essays and treatises. This is always the beauty of excellent fiction—it lets the author take complex themes and bring them to life within an environment of action and suspense.

Saga of the Well World is a powerful stimulus to many of the abstract faculties of the mind. These novels challenge our narrowmindedness and cultural prejudices, helping us go beyond them. Their themes are so well executed that reading them becomes a most enjoyable exercise in grasping the infinite and multidimensional nature of the universal mind—even for readers already used to working with abstract and symbolic thought.

It is a must for anyone interested in stretching his or her mind to embrace universal themes.

Explore Your Psychic World
by Ambrose & Olga Worrall

Ambrose and Olga Worrall were two of the most gifted psychics of our time, as well as two of the most respected healers. Each had the clairvoyant ability to communicate telepathically, to see auras, to converse with discarnates, and to heal people hundreds of miles away.

One of the things that made the Worralls so unique was their commitment to having their talents tested scientifically. Anyone who is tempted to claim that psychic skills and healing abilities have not been proven scientifically need only inquire into the extensive work done testing the Worralls throughout their lives. As an example of this commitment to scientific inquiry, Ambrose and Olga took part in a remarkable series of six seminars with scientists, medical doctors, and psychic investigators at Wainwright House in New York in the 1960's. This book is based on the insights presented by the Worralls during these seminars.

Explore Your Psychic World is one of the most thorough overviews of the psychic aspects of life in print today. It examines auras, astral travel, communication with discarnates, clairvoyance, possession, psychic attack, and dreams. This is not a recapitulation of what the Worralls had read on these topics; their insights come from their psychic observations.

Anyone interested in psychic phenomena will find *Explore Your Psychic World* to be both fascinating and enlightening.

The Great Divorce
by C.S. Lewis

The one great sin is separativeness—the deliberate act of estrangement from divine life. Whenever we put a gap between ourself and God, we cut ourself off from our true heritage.

C.S. Lewis understood the sin of alienation. In *The Great Divorce*, he wittily shows us just how easy it is to succumb to separativeness. This is not a story of broken marriages—it is an account of a bus trip from hell to heaven. The travellers are people who have earned a second chance of admittance to heaven.

Upon arriving in heaven, they are met by old friends and given every chance to stay permanently. In fact, they are never told they must leave. But for many of them, the force of their biases, fixed ideas, prejudices, and opinions is so strong that they do not find heaven to their liking. So they beat a hasty retreat to the bus and wait for it to take them back to hell.

Lewis reveals the biases and false assumptions of his characters with good humor and sharp satire, but the purpose of this book is not to make us laugh, although we certainly do. Lewis's purpose is to charm us into realizing that if we do not happen to be residing in heaven in our life, it is not heaven's fault. The fault lies entirely in our own separativeness.

To correct this problem, all that is necessary is to disown our separative attitudes and beliefs and begin living as though God dwells within us. Then we will discover that heaven truly is within us.

The Great Divorce is a wonderful story.

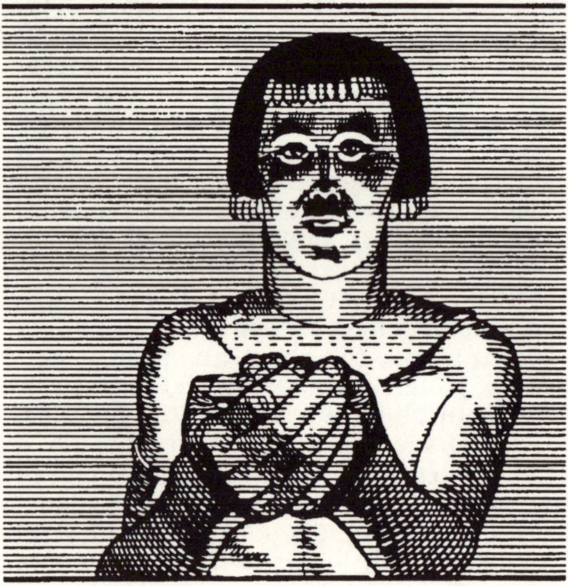

Forces of the Zodiac
by Robert R. Leichtman, M.D. & Carl Japikse

Each human being is influenced constantly by a wide variety of subtle forces. Most of us, however, are largely unaware of these forces—or their impact on our lives, problems, and opportunities. As a result, we are unable to act in life as effectively as we could.

The primary way in which humanity has sought to study these invisible influences on our lives has been through the science of astrology. Unfortunately, the practice of astrology has often been cheapened by people who have used it only to speculate about the future.

Forces of the Zodiac sets forth a brilliant new way of using astrological information. Written by Dr. Robert R. Leichtman and Carl Japikse, it is a practical guide to using the psychological and spiritual forces which are available to us to accelerate personal growth, expand our creativity, enrich relationships, strengthen leadership skills, solve problems, and seize opportunities.

According to the authors, this book is the result of six years of research, which began with the observation that certain trends, themes, and qualities influence everyone alike in each monthly sign of the zodiac—regardless of his or her natal sign. Everyone, for example, experiences a strong surge of aspiration and ambition each year when the sun is in Sagittarius—not just people born during that month.

For six years, Leichtman and Japikse intuitively studied and observed the changing forces. With their research completed, they took their findings and put them together, producing *Forces of the Zodiac.*

The book consists of a thorough description of astrological influences, what they mean to us, how to tune into them, and how we can harness them in our life. These preliminary chapters are then followed by 12 chapters of commentary describing how the forces of the 12 signs of the zodiac influence us.

Each chapter explores:

- The major archetypal forces which characterize one sign of the zodiac, and their divine purpose.
- The symbolism of the sign.
- How the major forces of the sign affect the average person, the spiritual aspirant, and the advanced person.
- The challenges of the sign to parents, friends, business, society, and spiritual aspiration.
- The problems of the sign.
- The opportunities of the sign.
- How to tune into the forces of the sign.

The book concludes with a chapter on what it means to use the forces of the zodiac as "companions of the soul." In fact, "companions of the soul" sums up one of the authors' primary themes, which is to demonstrate that these forces of the zodiac are living, dynamic energies which are vital parts of the divine creative effort. As such, our soul utilizes these forces on a regular basis, both in planning the direction of our life and our opportunities for growth and service. It regards them as its companions.

Forces of the Zodiac is a truly useful book—a book which should be our companion as we make our way through each month of the year.

The Initiation of the World
by Vera Stanley Alder

In her introduction, Vera Alder calls *The Initiation of the World* a different kind of history book than those usually found in schools—"*a golden history* which holds the key to a glorious future unfoldment."

And that is precisely what it is—a history not of wars, changes in government, and the rise and fall of empires, but rather a history of the development of the mind, the genius, and the spiritual nature of humanity. In short, easy-to-read chapters, Miss Alder tells the story of mankind's esoteric evolution.

Beginning with chapters on the growth of the mind and the plan of creation, she proceeds to examine the significance of the following themes in our cultural and spiritual development:

- Reincarnation.
- The seven rays.
- The Hierarchy.
- The path of initiation.
- The initiations of man.
- The great world teachers.

Using these themes, she then weaves an illuminating story about the birth of national genius and the initiation of the world as a whole. The result is a very provocative and intelligent examination of the concept of brotherhood—not as an utopian ideal but as a constant thread running throughout the *real* history of mankind, the impetus of human unfoldment.

This important book is must reading for anyone seeking a truer understanding of life on this planet.

The Unfinished Autobiography
by Alice A. Bailey

For 35 years, Alice A. Bailey worked in close, telepathic rapport with the master Djwahl Khul, writing 25 of the most profound books on the spiritual life, psychology, healing, and cosmology ever produced—from *Initiation, Human and Solar* to *The Reappearance of the Christ.*

It is easy to assume that anyone who could produce such a monumental opus must be a virtually indestructible person. And yet the strain on Mrs. Bailey was frequently great, as she stood at the forefront of human evolution.

Her *Unfinished Autobiography* is a candid portrait of her life and work—consistently witty, intellectually stimulating, and filled with revelations. It is, after all, not just the story of her life, but also the story of her bond with Djwhal Khul and her own master, Koot Hoomi. Yet for all the fascinating anecdotes about the masters, the real strength of Alice Bailey's autobiography is the human dimension it brings to spiritual service. Here, she chronicles the joys and rigors of a busy life and gives an inside look at the sacrifices involved in serving humanity.

It is an "unfinished" autobiography because Mrs. Bailey had envisioned four more sections. But in their place, there is fascinating material about the nature of her telepathic rapport with the Tibetan, a summary of her books, and the principles of esoteric teaching.

The Unfinished Autobiography is highly recommended.

Childhood's End
by Arthur C. Clarke

Just as the United States and Russia are about to launch the first rockets to the moon, enormous spaceships carrying "Overlords" appear over the major capitals of the world and begin issuing instructions to mankind. The Overlords do not actually appear on earth—they send their instructions through the secretary general of the United Nations—but they back up their orders with nonviolent yet effective demonstrations of great power.

Within a few years, they achieve a dramatic improvement in the course of civilization—although not without resistance from terrorists, religious fanatics, and nationalists. But the resistance is contained, and the real work of the Overlords on earth begins—the creation of a new race of "wonder children" who represent the next step in evolution for humanity.

These children are far superior to any human—and are even greater than the Overlords themselves. They have apparently transcended matter and are able to transmute it, which they do, in a scene of fiery transformation.

Childhood's End is a marvelously rich novel which introduces us to several significant themes: the idea that there is a Hierarchy of advanced humans who protect and guide the development of civilization and humanity; the rebelliousness of humanity toward its own destiny and purpose; and the ultimate transformation of human consciousness, leading to an entirely new race of God-like people.

This is Arthur Clarke at his best.

The Power of the Rays & Colour Meditations
by S.G.J. Ouseley

S.G.J. Ouseley has earned a reputation as the leading authority on the meaning and enlightened use of color. *The Power of the Rays* and *Colour Meditations* are his two most definitive statements on the subject.

Throughout both of these excellent books, Ouseley makes the point that he is referring to color as the life force symbolized by the hues of the spectrum. He leads us beyond the form of color to become aware of the quality of each color and the potent force associated with it.

These forces, he explains, can be highly useful in both meditative and healing work. In *The Power of the Rays*, he develops the "science of color healing," in which he describes the curative power of the seven major colors—and how to use them. In *Colour Meditations*, he explores the esoteric values of color and the use of these energies in meditation.

While the visualization of colors should never be considered a substitute for healing or meditative work, a true understanding of color, as presented in these two books, can be a highly useful adjunct to both healing and meditation. The key is to keep our priorities focused on establishing the right quality of consciousness, rather than the vivid image of a color.

Virtually all books written about color and color therapy are based on the work done by Ouseley. Yet none of the books that copy Ouseley's work is as good as these.

The Hidden Side of Things
by C.W. Leadbeater

What we see, hear, touch, and smell in the physical plane is only a fragment of God's creation. To live wisely and comprehend fully the nature of life, we must realize that there is a hidden side to reality, as well as an outer, tangible side. This inner side of life—indeed, the vast totality of life—is invisible to most of us. Yet it is often the key that unlocks the door to a true understanding of what is happening to us.

As C.W. Leadbeater puts it in his marvelous book, *The Hidden Side of Things*, it is as though we were people who were examining a huge tapestry in the process of being woven—from underneath the loom! From such a perspective, the unfolding tapestry would seem to be nothing but a confused mass of color and ragged threads, utterly lacking in order, beauty, meaning, or purpose. But if we could look at the tapestry from above, and with an understanding of the final design the weaver has in mind, we could see the reason for our confusion lies not in the tapestry, but in our limited, upside-down perspective.

The Hidden Side of Things is written to improve our perspective on life—to help us see life in its totality, not just in its physical aspect. It is a thorough exploration of the psychic dimensions of life and their impact on ordinary daily living, conducted by one of the greatest clairvoyants of the early twentieth century.

Bishop Leadbeater divides his investigation into three parts. The first is devoted to examining the psychic impact of the sun, the planets, our natural surroundings, and the thoughts of others upon us.

The second section explores the many ways in which we influence ourselves psychically—through the thoughts, feelings, and habits that we hold, and the environment we create around us. In the final part, Leadbeater deals with how we influence others psychically.

This is probably the best single volume in print about the influence of psychic energies and conditions on daily life. The Bishop writes from his own clairvoyant observation and experimentation, but with the constant goal of using these psychic insights to help us understand the confusing and mysterious aspects of living.

In writing about the invisible radiations of the sun, for example, Leadbeater shows us how these radiations affect our physical vitality and health. In describing the psychic emanations of physical objects, he examines how a knowledge of these emanations can be used productively, in choosing our personal possessions, making talismans, and so on.

There are several chapters on the ennobling influence of the magnetic emanations at sacred sites, cathedrals, museums, and consecrated places—and the impact of religious ceremonies. These locations and activities, the Bishop explains, exude unseen forces which stimulate the spiritual side of our nature—and can help us purify and enhance our consciousness. His first-hand reports make sense out of many mysterious rituals.

One of the major themes Leadbeater tackles is the subtle way in which we are influenced by other people—and mass consciousness as a whole. In particular, he examines the impact of prejudice, gossip, and deceit in public opinion.

The Bishop's strong statements on these topics might be upsetting to a person who has blandly assumed that his private thoughts are his own business and no one else's. But this is not the case, and Leadbeater clearly articulates the deadly and sometimes disgusting influence that strong negative feelings have on others—as seen clairvoyantly.

Having established this theme, he then expands upon it further, investigating the many ways in which the quality of our thoughts, feelings, and habits affect our own character and state of mind. The Bishop provides much food for thought—and a strong stimulus to discipline our behavior.

The Hidden Side of Things concludes with a thorough investigation of how we influence others—through good works we perform, the way we raise our children, collective thought, and our relationship with other kingdoms of life.

Bishop Leadbeater wrote many books in his lengthy career, and his collected writings represent one of the great sources of knowledge now available on the psychic dimensions of life. *The Hidden Side of Things* is probably Bishop Leadbeater's crowning achievement in describing the invisible nature of our lives. Every serious student can benefit from reading it.

The World Tree

An Encyclopedia of Traditional Symbols
by J.C. Cooper

The enlightened person knows that the language of every nation and people is something more than words and grammar. It is also the language of symbolism: the themes and images of its myths, heroes, religions, and civilization.

This is a language which speaks to us subconsciously, and so it is easy to miss its significance. But the intelligent person probes beyond the outer appearances of life, trying to understand the deeper significances that can be found at inner levels.

All of life is symbolic. As we learn to recognize this truth and become familiar with the symbolic language of our own culture—as well as the symbolic idiom of other cultures throughout the world—we greatly enrich our understanding of ourselves, our neighbors, our civilization, and the other peoples of the earth.

The problem is that sometimes it is hard to separate the personal and cultural meaning of symbols. This is where an in-depth reference book can be invaluable. One of the best is *An Illustrated Encyclopedia of Traditional Symbols* by J.C. Cooper.

This book is the work of intelligent scholarship and a thorough knowledge of cultural symbolism, making it vastly superior to the dream interpretation guides which have flooded the market recently. The entries are arranged alphabetically, making it easy to locate the meaning of symbols.

This is a marvelous book to thumb through, reading entries at random. But its real value is to use it as a guide to understanding the meanings of specific symbols that arise in dreams or meditations, or are encountered in books, plays, movies, art, music, or ceremonies.

Only the ignorant person dismisses these symbols as unimportant. The intelligent individual has long since discovered the enrichment which comes from pursuing their meanings—and tapping their archetypal force.

As Cooper writes: "Symbolism is basic to the human mind; to ignore it is to suffer a serious deficiency; it is fundamental to thinking."

The value of this volume is not that it makes a final statement on the meaning of any symbol, but that it helps start the thinking and interpretative process. It encourages us to put our minds to work to understand the symbolic patterns around us. It will serve the thinking person well throughout a lifetime of personal investigation.

As such, it is highly recommended as a cornerstone of any personal library or bookshelf.

God Always Says Yes
by Sue Sikking

"There is a great affirmative Power within every human form. There is an All-Knowing Presence within us that always says, 'Yes!' It is that something that has kept every man on the path toward some goal since the beginning of time. It is the power that fulfills our destiny, the spur to all progress."

So writes Sue Sikking in introducing the basic theme of this little gem—a book about each of us, our problems, and our relationship with God. We have the power to say both yes and no to the great possibilities of our life, she explains. But regardless of what we say, the divine presence within us always says yes.

If we desire something constructive, or try to treat others fairly, the inner power of the God within us helps us attain what our heart desires. But if we fear success, or worry about what others will do to us, we are also invoking our inner power, magnifying our negative desire.

The challenge is to break out of the ruts which trap us in downward spirals—and this is where *God Always Says Yes* shines. Mrs. Sikking offers suggestion after suggestion for breaking free from the limitation of our past, our failures, and our habits, so we may find and cultivate what she calls "a treasure in our heart."

Sue Sikking was for years the minister of one of the largest Unity churches in the country. She writes from her own rich experiences about using the power of the mind, linked with spirit, to overcome life's limitations and tragedies.

God Always Says Yes is a real treasure.

The Time Quartet
by Madeleine L'Engle

It is unusual that four of the best books written recently on the conflict of good and evil are children's stories. It is likewise unusual that four of the most mind-stretching books on the fourth dimension are children's stories. It is astonishing that these are the same four books.

The Time Quartet by Madeleine L'Engle is unusual. And excellent. These four novels richly deserve the awards they have won and their increasing popularity. Do not be sidetracked by the fact that these are children's books. Although unmistakably written for children, these books delight and enlighten adults, too.

All four books—*A Wrinkle in Time, A Wind in the Door, A Swiftly Tilting Planet,* and *Many Waters*—chronicle the adventures of the Murry family, primarily Meg and Charles Wallace. Meg is unusually bright and plucky, but Charles Wallace is something else. Even at five, at the start of the novels, his vocabulary and wisdom surpass that of most adults. And he has the habit of hobnobbing with beings from other galaxies.

In all four books, the Murry children are drawn into confrontations with the *Echthros*, the presence of evil in the universe. In each tale, they find different ways of conquering the Echthros, which is icy cold and prone to ripping holes in the sky. Anyone who has actually had to deal with the force of evil will realize the depth of insight contained in these four books. Much can be learned from these simple stories.

In *A Wrinkle in Time*, the children's father is

missing. He has been involved in a government experiment in tesseracting—traveling via the fourth dimension—and has been trapped by Echthroi (called It in this first story) on a dark planet. Charles Wallace, Meg, and her boyfriend Calvin are asked to rescue Mr. Murry—by three angels who appear in the form of dumpy but charming old ladies named Mrs. Whatsit, Mrs. Who, and Mrs. Which.

Taught to tesseract, the children manage to rescue Mr. Murry, but in the process, Charles Wallace becomes trapped by the It. It is up to Meg to return and face the evil in her young brother—icy cold and hard—and free him with a steadfast expression of love.

The theme of the redeeming value of love, and its power to defeat evil, is repeated in the second novel, *A Wind in the Door.* Charles Wallace is entering first grade and is intensely interested in mitochondria—intracellular organisms in the human body. And well he should be, for his own mitochondria are dying.

So is the universe; whole galaxies are disappearing. Once again, it is Meg, this time with the help of the cherubim Proginoskes, who must act to save her brother and the universe. Her adventures take her deep within the cells of Charles Wallace, through a form of intuitive rapport called *kything.* There, she learns the Echthroi are the problem; they are unnaming creation, stripping life of its identity.

To counter this danger, Meg learns to name creation as an act of love—a marvelous lesson in the value of selfhood and sacrifice.

The most epic of the four books is *A Swiftly Tilting Planet,* in which Charles Wallace travels back to crucial moments of history with Gaudior, a unicorn, to change the outcome of events, thus subtly averting the threat of dictatorship in the present. Meg stays behind, kything with her brother as he becomes four different people.

The plot is complex but extremely rich and powerful. Charles Wallace's primary weapon in this struggle with the Echthroi is a magical rune, which invokes the order of the heavens to stop the encroachment of evil.

Meg and Charles Wallace are grown up by the time of *Many Waters;* the action shifts to their twin brothers, Sandy and Dennys. They are "accidentally" tesseracted into the time of Noah, who is building the ark in anticipation of the "many waters." Caught up in a struggle of Biblical proportions, the twins struggle with the idea that God would actually destroy all life on earth with a flood, but gradually come to understand the underlying benevolence of seemingly incomprehensible divine acts—and discover, as their sister had before them, what it means to care. They likewise discover that neither time nor space can impede genuine love.

One of the most notable features of these stories is that the children are never saved by divine intervention; they triumph because they learn in the face of crisis, with divine help. This is a basic lesson of enlightenment.

It is also refreshing to encounter books in which intelligence and genius are treated with great respect and understanding. *The Time Quartet* is children's literature at its finest.

Scars of the Soul

by Mary Anne Woodward

Edgar Cayce was a remarkable psychic who, over a span of 40 years, gave almost 15,000 readings in a trance state, the majority of them for people with serious physical illnesses. Through these readings, he was able to discern the inner causes of disease and made an immense contribution to our understanding of the true nature of sickness and health.

Cayce did not view illness on just the physical level. To him, many physical ailments were the direct result of character flaws and defects carried over from earlier lifetimes. These he discussed in terms of *karma*—the esoteric principle of consequences or continuity. Quite simply, we carry the good and bad issues of our character with us as we make our life along the path. As we reinvest the good in new applications of our skills and talents, it grows and becomes more abundant. It promotes good health. Conversely, as we repeatedly indulge in the bad, and fail to transform it into something more spiritual, it cuts its groove in our character more deeply. Sooner or later, it restricts our health—and may even threaten our livingness.

Cayce referred to the deeper, more malignant "grooves" etched in our character as "scars of the soul"—not that they are actually of the soul, but that they obscure the light of the soul from shining into our character. Inspired by this phrase and her lifelong study of Cayce, Mary Anne Woodward has put together a new book on Cayce, karma, and holistic healing, aptly titled *Scars of the Soul*.

In many ways, this new book is a companion volume to Ms. Woodward's earlier book, *Edgar Cayce's Story of Karma*. In other ways, however, it is more specifically focused, filled with valuable insights into the origin of disease.

The first few chapters explain the concept of karma and how karmic trends develop from life to life. The meat of the book, however, is the third chapter, which covers more than half the text and presents case after case in which Cayce commented on their karmic antecedents.

The range of diseases on which Cayce commented is truly impressive. The cases Ms. Woodward chose to examine begin with cancer and make their way through stroke, paralysis, diabetes, tuberculosis, arthritis, asthma, acne, allergies, anemia, birth defects, epilepsy, multiple sclerosis, Parkinson's, alcoholism, and even accidents and homosexuality. It is fascinating to read the way in which Cayce handled this wide diversity of illnesses. Whenever possible, he devoted the majority of his comments to practical steps which could be taken to alleviate the pain and suffering of the diseased condition, but he likewise attempted to show as clearly as possible the underlying psychological problems which gave rise to the difficulty—and what could be done to correct them.

A case of epilepsy, for instance, is traced back to a lifetime (probably a series of lives) in which the individual lusted to control and dominate others for his own self-aggrandizement, almost to the point of possession. A case of cancer is traced to a lifetime in which the person mocked the suffering of others—Christians being persecuted for their faith.

In the first case, the person was trapped in

the disease; no tangible improvement was reported. In the second, a conscious effort was made to alter the character flaws that induced the karma, and the "incurable" was cured.

Many of the cases examined in this book are less life threatening, yet nonetheless instructive. In one in particular, a young man was suffering from multiple sclerosis and eventually went blind. Cayce chided him for being selfish and filled with malice and told him the outcome of his physical condition would depend on inner changes: "When the body becomes so self-satisfied, so self-centered as to renounce, refuse, or does not change its attitude, so long as there is hate, malice, injustice.... there cannot be healing to that condition of this body....What would the body be healed for? That it might add to its own selfishness? Then it had better remain as it is."

It is in comments such as these that the real value of *Scars of the Soul* lies. Time after time, Cayce hits the important themes of health squarely on target. It is clear that he understood that it is not a condition from 5,000 years ago which prevents us from enjoying good health today, even though it may have cast the pattern for our problem. It is our unwillingness to grow and become a mature person, by changing our character, that keeps us trapped in ill health— even for 5,000 years!

The one weak area of the book is the final chapter on the use of meditation to change karmic patterns; the description of meditation is too simplistic and filled with clichés of spiritual growth to be of much real help. But if this last chapter is skipped, most people will find *Scars of the Soul* enlightening.

The Hour Glass
by Carl Japikse

The fable has long been a favorite device for conveying esoteric truths as well as entertaining and delighting readers. *The Hour Glass* is a collection of fables spun in the inventive mind of Carl Japikse.

But these are fables with a *difference*, for each one contains a grain of sand which, as it trickles through the hour glass of an inquiring mind, magically transforms itself into a growing seed of new understanding—about time, conflict, wisdom, creativity, ingenuity, pride, courage, and the most fundamental themes of human living. They are fables that will charm children, but *enlighten* adults.

This delightful set of stories embraces a wide range of fabulous characters—from an artistic donkey and an intellectual coyote to a politicking baboon and a messianic minnow. There are even a few fables about men and women—60 fables in all, one for each minute the sands of the hour glass mark as they tumble on their journey through time.

Many of the fables are written so that they may be used as a focus for our contemplative thinking or meditation. As such, they are really parables revealing something of divine life, as well as fables commenting on the foibles and foolishness of human life. As might be expected, one of Japikse's favorite themes is the esoteric potential of time.

The fables are accompanied by 21 drawings by Mark Peyton. *The Hour Glass* is a refreshing, original collection.

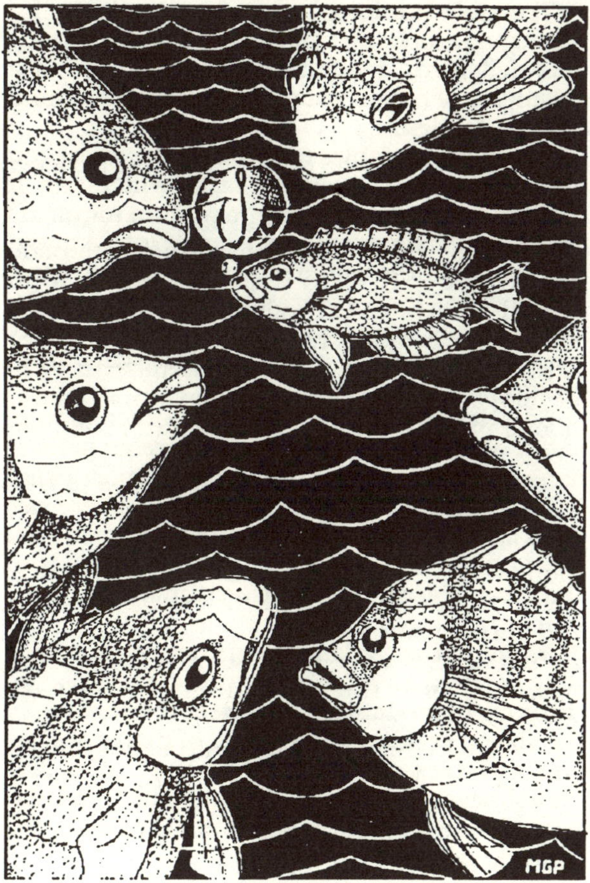
MGP

The World of Null-A
by A.E. van Vogt

Gilbert Gosseyn is not the person he thought he was. In fact, no one seems to know exactly who he is. And, since he is caught up in the middle of a plot to commit intergalactic genocide against the Earth, quite a few people would like to know just who he is—including Gosseyn himself.

It is after his enemies kill him, and Gosseyn reemerges a month later in a duplicate body, that Gosseyn realizes that his identity is not linked to his physical body. Nor can he assume it is to be found in his thoughts, values, and attitudes, since he cannot remember how he developed them. As a result, he launches into a long process of self-examination, leaving no preconception unturned.

Eventually, he develops a measure of telepathic communication which draws him into rapport with the scientist of whom he is a clone—at the same moment that he is able to defeat the forces that seek to destroy the world.

This is a completely new edition of *The World of Null-A*, one of the great science fiction classics of all time. The title derives from the basic premise that the advanced thinkers of the time, 600 years in the future, have all been trained in non-Aristotelian thinking—null-A, for short. But as perceptive as Gosseyn is, even his null-A training is insufficient to decipher his puzzling situation. He must go a step further and develop the psychic potentials of his mind.

Fast-paced and full of action, *The World of Null-A* deserves its excellent reputation.

The Players of Null-A
by A.E. van Vogt

Poor Gilbert Gosseyn. He does not even have time to savor the smashing victory he scored at the end of *The World of Null-A*. For as soon as Enro the Red learns of his defeat in the solar system, he steps up his egomaniacal drive to become dictator of the whole universe. And once more Gosseyn is thrust smack into the middle of the action—the only man capable of stopping Enro and bringing his reign of terror to an end.

To achieve victory, however, Gosseyn must use both of his minds—and he must learn to trust in the unseen wisdom of the greater intelligence that is moving him willy-nilly, like a player in a cosmic game, throughout the universe. At times, Gosseyn is in his own body; at other times, he is in the body of Prince Ashargin, whom Enro is grooming to be a puppet leader. It is only when Gosseyn learns to project his consciousness at will that he discovers the key that leads him again to triumph.

The Players of Null-A is a fast-moving action packed science fiction tale by A.E. van Vogt that completes the story begun in *The World of Null-A*. But this is one instance in which the sequel is every bit as exciting as the original.

As he did in *The World of Null-A*, van Vogt adroitly crafts a story that reminds us that the potential for developing the human mind and the power of its awareness far exceeds the potential of technology—and that the key to self-mastery lies, as it always has, in refining our skills in thinking and acting intelligently.

Magister Ludi
by Hermann Hesse

The Glass Bead Game is a sophisticated mental encounter played by the finest minds of the 25th century. The game draws on all human knowledge, all facets of culture, and unifies it, revealing the underlying harmony of the universal mind—and the capacity of the noble human mind to tap it and interact with it.

Joseph Knecht is a brilliant student who rises to become "Magister Ludi"—the master of the Glass Bead Game. Yet Knecht is disturbed by the conventions of the game. In an effort to cultivate pure knowledge—pure culture and pure science—the game players have become oddly detached from society. They have fallen victim to the glamour of the ivory tower, believing that knowledge exists for its own sake, rather than to serve human and divine evolution.

Ultimately, Knecht relinquishes his post as master of the Game, forced by his own destiny to return to an active life. And in so doing, he demonstrates what it means to be alive in the world. We must have knowledge, but we must act on the knowledge we have, and serve life. If we train our mind sufficiently, we can gain archetypal knowledge—knowledge of the basic patterns of all creation. But once we know these things, we must activate them and translate them into achievements which help humanity and God.

Magister Ludi is a powerful novel. It sets before us a grand vista of what the mind can become, then teaches us what it means for anyone—and humanity as a whole—to grow.

Your Power To Be
by J. Sig Paulson

"The greatest power in the universe is the power to be! It expresses itself in every created thing. A drop of water, a blade of grass, a planet, a star, a dog, a cat, a bird, are all expressions of the power to be. It is in man that the power to be finds its greatest expression and its greatest potential....Man is an instrument capable of infinite expansion as he awakens to his true identity and accepts his place in the divine scheme of things."

So writes J. Sig Paulson in *Your Power To Be*, one of the most practical books in print on putting the power of spirit to work in our life. Paulson, a Unity minister in Texas, chides the churches for failing to teach their members about the spiritual light within themselves and what it means to express it through acts of love and wisdom. He then goes on to remedy the situation, presenting a drill in self-realization followed by a thorough description of our 13 powers to be—light, faith, will, understanding, imagination, enthusiasm, love, authority, wisdom, joy, strength, forgiveness, and life.

As Paulson puts it, *Your Power To Be* is a book for "the spiritually adventurous, those who are ready to walk the largely uncharted paths of their own souls." And what a great adventure it is! In a very real sense, it is an adventure into light itself—an adventure into the inner realms of human *and* divine consciousness and what can be done with it, to improve the quality of our lives and better serve God.

Your Power To Be is a book filled with light.

The Spiritual Fitness Handbook
by David R. Houston

Here's a little book that many people will find to be an invaluable companion in their effort to tread the spiritual path. It's a gem of simplicity, yet filled with insights that steadily enrich us.

Author David Houston's goal is to help each of us become spiritually fit—in harmony with the spirit within us. His emphasis is focused, therefore, on practicing those things which promote spiritual health, while learning to abstain from anything which undermines our spiritual fitness and well-being. But don't get the wrong idea. This is not a book of rules for the spiritual aspirant. It is more a set of observations which have worked for Houston—and will work just as well for anyone who makes a serious effort to use them. They make sense.

The charm of this book is that Houston helps us learn these things without preaching at us or lecturing us. He leads us gently step by step into a comprehensive examination of who we are, what we believe, and how we confuse ourself. He helps us break down the walls of glamour and illusion we have erected around us. But instead of being pompous, as so many spiritual writers can be, he makes the journey fun. This is, after all, a journey that liberates us from what traps and limits us. What could be more joyful?

The Spiritual Fitness Handbook is highly recommended as an important tool for the self-examined life.

Stranger in a Strange Land

by Robert Heinlein

The stranger is Valentine Michael Smith. The strange land is Earth, where Smith, a Martian, inhabits a human body. It is hard for Smith to comprehend the strange ways of humans—strange ways such as sex, religion, and laughter. He is more at home with the customs of "grokking" and "sharing water."

The humans, of course, have as much difficulty, even more so, understanding the ways of Smith—his ability to levitate, to stop objects in midair, and to communicate telepathically.

The effort of Smith to understand humans and the efforts of his friends to understand him create an outstanding story—consistently funny, unrelentingly satiric, and filled with brilliant insights into what it means to *expand consciousness.* In the end, however, it is not Smith's Martian heritage that makes him a stranger in a strange land, but his rapport with humans. He taps the essence of the human experience—he groks in fullness—and seeks to share it with others, only to be rejected by those who fear their own humanity, their own divinity.

In this way, Heinlein shows us that we become strangers in a strange land whenever we fail to tap the fullness of our humanity. Of course, we could help our cause by learning to grok. And Valentine Michael Smith is just the one to teach us how.

Stranger in a Strange Land is "must reading."

Occult Medicine Can Save Your Life
by C. Norman Shealy, M.D.

"There is a magic in medicine, there always has been—and this is why medical miracles are a recognized and well-documented aspect of professional practice and medical care. Perhaps that magic is love energy, perhaps it's faith—for certainly no patient has ever been helped or cured or healed unless he has had faith in what his doctor is doing for him. In any case, the doctors' task today is to put that magic—that faith—back into medicine where it belongs, to learn to make the miracles available for the patient when nothing else can help!"

So writes C. Norman Shealy, M.D. in *Occult Medicine Can Save Your Life*—a thorough evaluation of nonmedical forms of healing and therapy, from acupuncture and etheric surgery to psychic diagnosis, spiritual healing, and astrology. Shealy's goal is to alert the reader to ways in which these "occult" or metaphysical practices can be used together with modern medicine, to speed the healing process.

Along the way, Dr. Shealy also frankly discusses the limitations of some practices of conventional medicine, especially the use of drugs and surgery. He writes eloquently of the holistic approach to health.

Dr. Shealy is founder of the world-famous Pain and Health Rehabilitation Center in Springfield, Missouri. *Occult Medicine Can Save Your Life* is must reading for anyone interested in the full meaning of health.

Far Memory
by Joan Grant

"Far memory" is the ability to recall one's earlier lifetimes with as much clarity and vividness as one might recall an episode from 20 years ago in this lifetime. Joan Grant had an exceptional talent for far memory—a talent she developed as a young adult. Then, a "chance" encounter with four Egyptian scarabs brought a number of specific lifetimes into unusually sharp focus, leading to the writing of seven novels which are, in fact, recollections of earlier lives she has led, from ancient Egypt to Renaissance Italy, from thousands of years ago in America to the birth of the Roman Empire.

The best known of these novels, *Winged Pharaoh*, became an immediate bestseller when first published in 1937—and still remains popular today, fifty years later, as do the other novels which were subsequently released.

Far Memory is Joan's autobiography. In it, Joan tells the story of her childhood and young adult life, and how she came to develop her intuitive skills and write her novels. It is a fascinating, even breathtaking story to read, as she recounts her adventures as a high-spirited child, the shock of losing her fiance through an accident, encounters with H.G. Wells, Aleister Crowley, and Sir Oliver Lodge, and, ultimately, the unfoldment of her amazing skills. In many ways, Joan's present life is as stirring as any earlier one.

Far Memory is a joy to read—and is filled with marvelous descriptions of what it means to develop real psychic talent.

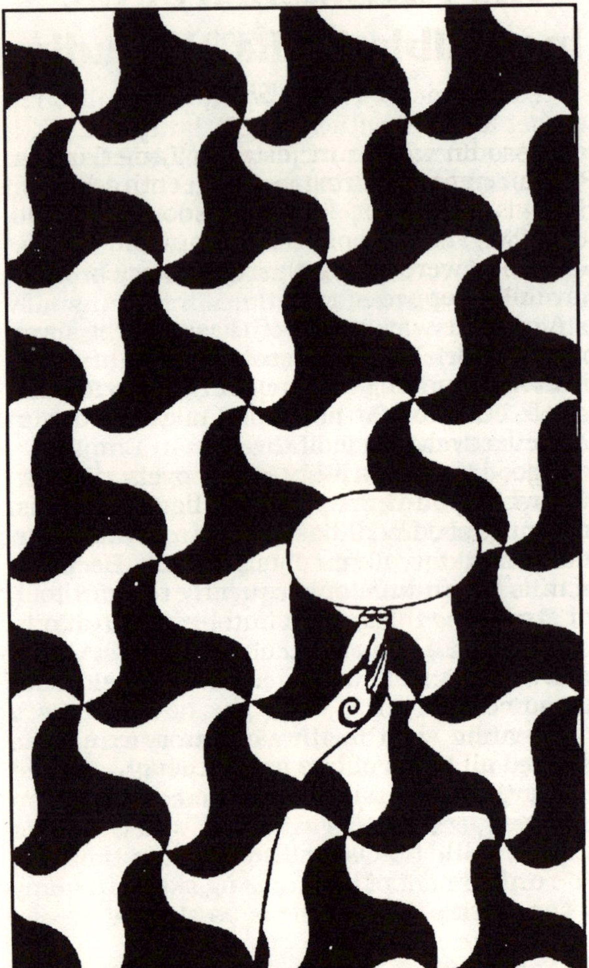

The Pleasantries of the Incredible Mulla Nasrudin
by Idries Shah

Nasrudin was court jester to Tamerlane, a Persian emperor during the fourteenth century. His wise jests—or foolish wisdom—became legendary, and people throughout the Middle East soon were telling Nasrudin stories. They have not stopped since.

Along the way, many of these stories have become enriched with esoteric insights and overtones, making them not only funny stories to tell, but thought-provoking tales to ponder on, reflectively or meditatively.

A good Nasrudin story is a slippery delight; just when you think you have figured out its meaning, you find it has at least a dozen other interpretations, all equally significant. Because of this, Nasrudin stories are an excellent tool for stretching the imagination—and intuition.

Idries Shah has collected the best of the Nasrudin stories and added a few of his own. Here are some:

Nasrudin went to the shop of a man who stocked all kinds of bits and pieces.

"Have you got nails?" he asked.

"Yes."

"And leather, good leather?"

"Yes."

"And twine?"

"Yes."

"And dye?" "Yes."

"Then why, for Heaven's sake, don't you make a pair of boots?"

A Sampling of Nasrudin

Nasrudin was sitting among the branches of a tree, sniffing the blossoms and sunning himself. A traveller asked him what he was doing there.

"Climbing the Great Pyramid."

"You are nowhere near a pyramid. And there are four ways up a pyramid: one by each face. That is a tree!"

"Yes," said Nasrudin. "But it's much more fun like this, don't you think? Birds, blossoms, zephyrs, sunshine. I hardly think I could have done better."

A philosopher, having made an appointment to dispute with Nasrudin, called and found him away from home.

Infuriated, he picked up a piece of chalk and wrote "Stupid Oaf" on Nasrudin's gate.

As soon as he got home and saw this, Nasrudin rushed to the philosopher's house.

"I had forgotten," he said, "that you were to call. And I apologize for not being home. Of course, I remembered the appointment as soon as I saw that you had left your name on my door."

Nasrudin's wife heard a tremendous thump outdoors, and ran to investigate.

"Nothing to worry about," said Nasrudin, "It was only my cloak which fell to the ground."

"What, and made a noise like that?"

"Yes, I was inside it at the time."

The Call to the Heights
by Geoffrey Hodson

In ancient times, spiritual instruction was given in mystery schools or temples. Today, even though such schools do not exist physically, the same kind of instruction is available—to anyone who answers "the call to the heights."

This is the basic message of Geoffrey Hodson's book, *The Call To The Heights*, quite possibly the most comprehensive of all the books this great clairvoyant wrote. In it, he outlines with clarity the steps involved in treading the spiritual path and opening the doorway to illumination.

Even though the mystery schools exist only at inner levels now, Hodson makes it very clear that they are more accessible than ever. He then proceeds to explain what we must do to discover our own connections to these inner sources. In specific, he describes the changes we must make in order to respond to the call to the heights—the pitfalls and glamours to avoid and the qualities to be acquired. In presenting these ideas, Hodson manages to convey a great deal of esoteric insight about the rays, discipleship, and initiation.

The result is a thoroughly modern explanation of the ancient wisdom—a rare and important achievement. But Hodson does not content himself with personal growth. Some of the best chapters are those he devotes to describing the nature of the emerging global consciousness which attends spiritual growth. He points out how important it is for each of us to become a world disciple.

This is a "call" none of us should ignore.

The Secret Path
by Paul Brunton

"True vision is a tremendous experience, not a set of theories. No man who has ever lived through even a temporary spiritual experience is ever likely to forget it."

So writes Paul Brunton in *The Secret Path*, his remarkable commentary on the process of contacting our Overself or soul, and how this contact enriches our life. After several years of being out of print, this classic is now available in a new edition—and deservedly so.

Paul Brunton was one of the first-rate thinkers of the 20th century—an excellent writer who tapped the inner reservoirs of spirit and then described it in his many books. But he did not write for the mystic; he wrote instead for the average intelligent person who is caught up in the struggle to make the world a better place in which to live and work and prosper—in particular, for men and women of business, practical affairs, and worldly responsibilities.

The Secret Path is written very much in this spirit, as a guide which is meant to reveal the power of the soul to replenish our physical, mental, and spiritual strength, thereby renewing us for the tasks and challenges of daily life. It is designed to lead us into a direct, not a theoretical, relationship with our real self.

Indeed, one of the continuing themes of *The Secret Path* is its emphasis on self-transformation. Over and over, Brunton stresses the power of spirit to change our habits, thoughts, and attitudes—and shows us how. This is one of those rare books that *can* change lives.

The Boy Who Saw True

Most diaries given to children as Christmas presents become treasure troves of their deepest feelings and most private secrets, and the diary published as *The Boy Who Saw True* is no exception. Rather, it is the boy who wrote it who was exceptional.

"Seeing true" is the capacity to see clairvoyantly, and this delightful book is the actual diary of a small boy with clairvoyant gifts growing up in Victorian England. Published anonymously in 1953 after the author's death as an adult, *The Boy Who Saw True* records the tribulations of growing up psychic in a family with absolutely no appreciation for psychic abilities.

"I was too in the dumps to write my diary last night," the lad reports on Feb. 19, 1885. "When Mildred and I came back from Arnold's where we'd been asked to tea, we went to speak to mamma in the morning room, and I saw Uncle Willie sitting in papa's chair and smiling at us. And just then papa came back from bizzness, and after he had kissed us all, was going to sit down, when I cried, 'Don't sit there, Uncle Willie is sitting in that chair.' And mamma looked all funny, and said, 'I rarely don't know what we're going to do with that child,' and papa said, very cross, 'What are you talking about, boy? Why, your Uncle Willie has been dead these two years.' Then he told Mildred to take me upstairs at once."

Only slowly does the boy come to learn that not everyone can see spirits, auras, gnomes, fairies, and other psychic realities as he can—in fact, almost no one can. He also learns not to talk about what he sees clairvoyantly with his family members, who only ridicule or punish him for it. Instead, he pours his observations into his diary. The result is a truly remarkable chronicle of genuine psychic gifts and their development.

The entries were edited by the author shortly before his death, but have been left in their original form, complete with the spelling errors, grammar mistakes, and innocent gaffes a small boy would make. This also preserves the full spirit, charm, and humanity with which they were written. And this is one of the great features of the book: it is not a dry textbook on psychic realities or the spiritual life, but a vivid, *living* account of life as seen through penetrating, clear seeing eyes. It is both entertaining to read and profoundly insightful—a rare combination indeed.

As the boy realizes that no one in his family can understand him, he builds a strong bond with his Uncle Willie and his grandfather, both of whom are in spirit. They comfort him in his bewilderment, guide him through several crises, and introduce him to some basic ideas about the inner planes.

At one point, for example, the boy asks his grandfather why his grandmother never comes to visit as he does. "And he said something about spirits getting thought-bound like birds getting egg-bound, and made us laugh because it seemed such a funny thing to say. He told us that while the grandmater was still on earth, she reckoned, same as a lot of people do, that she and a few others who thought exactly as she did were the only people what were going to be saved. 'And now,' said grandpa, 'she lives in a world of thoughts which she and others have created with their own fallacious convictions.'"

Slowly, the boy's world expands. He is assigned a tutor who is impressed by his psychic abilities and begins to study them with an open mind. He encourages the boy to conduct various experiments psychically, and this provides some of the most interesting material in the book. Later, the boy makes the acquaintance, psychically, of an "Elder Brother" and some of his disciples, who teach the lad about his psychic gifts and the spiritual life. These teachings are also recorded in the diary, providing an unusual glimpse into the support and instruction given by a Master to a spiritual aspirant.

Perhaps most significantly, however, this book is a candid account of the problems closed-mindedness can create, especially in raising children. Talented children often have a difficult time in growing up, because their talents separate them from other children and many adults. This is particularly true when the talents are psychic gifts. Many people are so sure of their own opinions that they instantly reject all evidence to the contrary, even when the evidence comes from the observations of an honest little boy.

The heroes of this book are the ones who help the boy understand himself, his talents, and the world around him. They stand out clearly from those with closed minds, who constantly fail to accept the lad for what he is.

The Boy Who Saw True is an important contribution to psychic literature. It is highly recommended—to parents, to children, and to everyone interested in the inner dimensions of life.

The Chronicles of Narnia
by C.S. Lewis

Narnia is a magical land inhabited by talking animals and trees, powerful evil, magic, and spiritual forces. Four children enter Narnia through a huge wardrobe closet and become entangled in the struggles of Narnia—the struggle of the power of good to triumph over evil.

The seven books in *The Chronicles of Narnia* have come to be viewed as classics of children's fantasy, and they can indeed be read at that level. But Lewis wrote these tales for adults as well—adults with eyes that see and ears that hear.

The chronicles are really an ingenious fable of the magic of divine order and the redeeming power of spirit, as it is embodied in the form of a Christ-like lion, Aslan. In order to fulfill an ancient prophecy, Aslan sacrifices himself for the children and allows himself to be slain in their stead—only to resurrect himself and become the central presence of these tales.

The adventures of Narnia continue, each illustrating an important facet of our personal struggles to live up to our divine potential, until the final book, in which the inhabitants enter a stable where Aslan is said to reside. Inside, each finds what he has created in his expectations. Those who have lived an illusion find their illusions, but those who have learned to see spiritually find a wonderful new land. And from inside the stable, they see that Narnia is ceasing to be.

All spiritual adults will treasure these marvelous and magical stories.

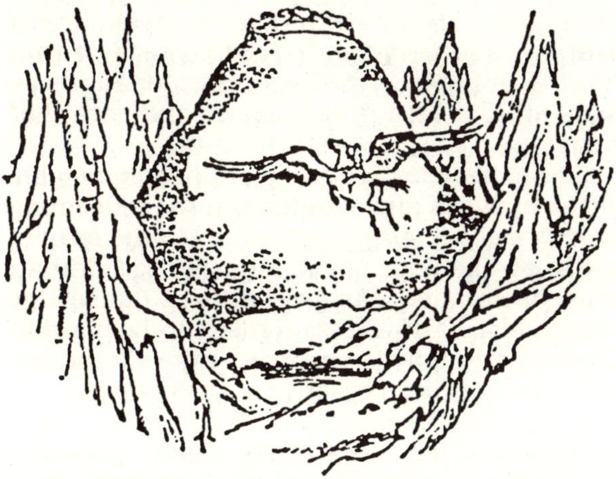

Driving Your Own Karma
by Swami Beyondananda

Driving Your Own Karma, a new book on the spiritual path, will take you on the wildest, funniest ride you've been on for a long time. Subtitled "Swami Beyondananda's Tour Guide to Enlightenment," it is Steve Bhaerman's latest contribution to good humor along the Path.

The book is a blend of lessons from the Swami plus letters from his "students." After training a group of students in what he called "The Incompletion Seminar," for instance, the Swami received letters such as: "Dear Swami, Love your training! And the thing I love most is—hey, listen—it's been good talking to you. I'll write some other time—Lou Sends."

The Swami deals with almost every fad of spiritual growth, advocating the use of Tantrum Yoga to heat your home with anger, describing how Fundamentalism puts the Fun ahead of the Mental, and teaching us how we can use Auto-Suggestion Techniques to maintain our car.

This book is guaranteed to brighten the burdens of the spiritual path. My favorite chapter is on "Looking out for Number Two," in which the Swami tells us what to do to treat Emotion Sickness. He claims to base his teachings on the ancient texts of Confusionism, which sounds about right. And for those who are slow learners, he concludes the chapter by asking: "Feeling Too Good Lately? Well, my friends, if your answer is yes, then you need Swami Beyondananda's new seminar, now on cassette tape, 'Guilt: Where To Get It, How To Keep It.'"

The Secret Life of the Unborn Child

by Thomas Veny, M.D.

The world of the unborn child is like a different dimension to us—dark, mysterious, something we cannot directly participate in. And most adults treat it as such. They regard the unborn fetus as unfeeling, unknowing, and unconscious.

Thomas Verny, M.D. has compiled an amazing amount of research that convincingly suggests that this just is not true. According to Dr. Verny, unborn children are:

- Capable of learning.
- Able to warn parents and doctors of medical problems they may not be aware of.
- Able to hear and respond to voices and sounds—even music.
- Able to distinguish between pleasant, classical music and discordant music such as hard rock.
- Sensitive to the feelings of their parents.
- Capable of responding to love.

These findings and more are the results of six years of study of unborn and newly-born children by psychiatrist Verny. They are compiled in his remarkable new book, *The Secret Life of the Unborn Child.*

This is an important book, not just for would-be parents but for anyone interested in understanding the nature of consciousness, the structure of our personal psychology, and the psychic capacities of the human being. Reading this book may also be a startling revelation for anyone who has struggled with confusing conflicts, likes and dislikes, and fears. It is amazing how many of these problems can actually be imprinted *prior to birth.*

Dr. Verny tells his story with charm and style, spicing the book with marvelous anecdotes such as the story of conductor Boris Brott who, early in his career, found that he often knew the cello parts of certain pieces he was conducting sight unseen. This fascinated him, so he told his mother, a professional cellist. She asked him to name the pieces in which this had happened. He did—and they all turned out to be pieces she had been rehearsing while she *was pregnant with Boris!* He had not only heard the music his mother was practicing, but had memorized every detail of it.

The real value of this book, however, lies not in its anecdotes but in its revelations and implications. One of the most important points Dr. Verny makes, for example, is that the unborn child is alive and aware of its environment. It is aware of the thoughts and feelings of its parents and other influences even before actual sensory organs have been developed in the fetus. In fact, the character of the newborn child is strongly influenced by the thoughts and feelings of the parents, especially the mother, during the entire time of pregnancy. Dr. Verny recounts case after case of children growing up with feelings of rejection because they were unwanted pregnancies.

On the other hand, he also presents strong evidence that babies who are praised and loved while still in utero become well-adjusted children and adults. Although Dr. Verny does not specifically discuss these phenomena in terms of psychic communication, it is clear that the perceptions of the unborn child are psychic. In particular, he states that the unborn child is very sensitive to deep-seated patterns of parental emotion.

In this manner, *The Secret Life of the Unborn Child* presents a wealth of evidence that the psychic environment in which we live has a strong influence in shaping our consciousness. It stands to reason that if psychic influences are so strong on the unborn child, they must also be powerful factors on us after we are born.

In personal conversations, Dr. Verny takes this theme further than he dared to in print. He is personally convinced that the unborn child is psychically aware what its parents think about it, their general emotional state, and the major events going on in the "outside world." He is also convinced that the unborn child is influenced by past lives, and reports that young children will often consciously remember episodes from earlier lives up to the age of four.

Even though these findings are not reported in the book, Dr. Verny does make a strong case for them indirectly, stating that science can no longer ignore the evidence of an "extraneurological memory system" and "sympathetic" communication. In this way, he shatters one of the great mental blocks of science—the belief that consciousness is grounded exclusively in the physical system.

The Secret Life of the Unborn Child is not just a study of the first nine months of human life, but it is more than this as well. It is a landmark book which deserves to be read by everyone interested in knowing more about how we think, feel, and learn.

And the Devil Will Drag You Under
by Jack L. Chalker

Suppose the universe is actually a vast laboratory experiment created by a group of unimaginably powerful beings—and that the laws of physics and human behavior are just the creation of the Department of Probabilities of a celestial university, as part of a research project. And suppose earth is about to be destroyed by a colliding asteroid. This is the premise of *And The Devil Will Drag You Under*.

Mac Walters and Jill McCullough are two humans recruited by the "supervisor" of earth to save the planet from destruction. Their mission is to travel to five alternate universes and steal five magic jewels, presumably so the supervisor can save earth.

Each of the five universes is a different experiment. In one, divine law and justice are immediate, painful, and automatic. In another, there are no rules; those with the strongest minds and wills rule everyone else. As Mac and Jill journey through these strange dimensions, they learn to adapt—and they also learn how important free will, individuality, and a sense of inner morality are. Ultimately, Mac and Jill are successful in obtaining the five jewels. It is then that we learn that the "supervisor" is not what he claimed to be, as the genuine order of the universe acts swiftly to prevent him from grabbing control of the whole system.

And The Devil Will Drag You Under is top notch science fiction.

The Secrets of Dr. Taverner
by Dion Fortune

"My chief interest lies in those regions of psychology which orthodox science has not as yet ventured to explore. If you work with me you will see some queer things, but all I ask of you is, that you should keep an open mind and a shut mouth."

With these words, Dr. Taverner introduces himself to Dr. Rhodes, whom he is hiring to be his assistant at the nursing home he runs. But this is not a conventional nursing home. It is a hospital for all manner of unorthodox mental disturbances, from psychic attack to disruptions in group minds to vampirism.

To this nursing home come the most bizarre cases of psychic disability and confusion. Dr. Rhodes applies all that he knows from conventional psychology—but it is consistently inadequate. Only the secret knowledge of Taverner, based on a thorough occult training, is enough to unravel the solutions.

The cases in *The Secrets of Dr. Taverner* are presented as individual short stories, 12 in all. Although written as fiction, and every bit as gripping and entertaining as the stories of Sherlock Holmes, the stories are based on actual cases. Dion Fortune states that "Taverner" and his nursing home did exist, and the stories have not in any way been exaggerated in transposing them into fiction.

For anyone interested in learning more about human nature and the psychic realities of life, *The Secrets of Dr. Taverner* is an unparalleled treasure of esoteric fiction.

Thought-Forms
by Annie Besant & C.W. Leadbeater

"Each definite thought produces a double effect—a radiating vibration and a floating form," write the authors of *Thought-Forms*. "The thought itself appears first to clairvoyant sight as a vibration in the mental body, and this may be either simple or complex."

Examining these thought-forms and vibrations, both in their simple and their complex arrangements, is the purpose of *Thought-Forms*, unquestionably the most authoritative statement on the subject in print. Annie Besant and C.W. Leadbeater were both outstanding clairvoyants in the early decades of this century, and this book is a record of their observations of the nature of thoughts and emotions.

One of the virtues of this book is that it is richly illustrated, in color, with drawings based on the observations of the authors. In addition to reading about the difference between grief and joy, for instance, we can see it for ourselves.

The insights presented in this way are both stunning and illuminating. The authors examine the meaning of color and the vibratory nature of thought, then go on to case after case example of the psychic nature of affection, devotion, anger, fear, greed, and sympathy, as well as a detailed examination of the kind of thought-forms produced during meditation, those produced by healing or kind thoughts directed at others, and those generated by music.

All in all, this is one of the most fascinating books on clairvoyance in print.

From Bethlehem to Calvary
by Alice A. Bailey

The initiations of the spiritual path are, by their very nature, a great mystery—one which is often confusing, yet usually quite appealing, to the spiritual aspirant. As a result, a lot of nonsense and misinformation has been written about initiation, and many people have formed fanciful beliefs of what it entails.

From Bethlehem to Calvary is a practical commentary on the mysteries of initiation—one that all spiritual aspirants will find extremely helpful. Alice Bailey compares the five major initiations of the spiritual path with five important events in the life of the Christ—thereby helping us better understand the symbolic meaning of these episodes as well as the true meaning of initiation. The five initiations are:

1. The Birth at Bethlehem.
2. The Baptism in the Jordan.
3. The Transfiguration.
4. The Crucifixion.
5. The Resurrection and Ascension.

One by one, these episodes from the life of Christ are examined from the perspective of how Jesus was initiated into a greater range of understanding, enlightenment, and service. But this is not really a book about Jesus—it is a book about each of us who aspires to initiation. It is written to be used by the spiritual aspirant to understand the changes which must be made in his or her life in order to serve a larger role in the life of mankind.

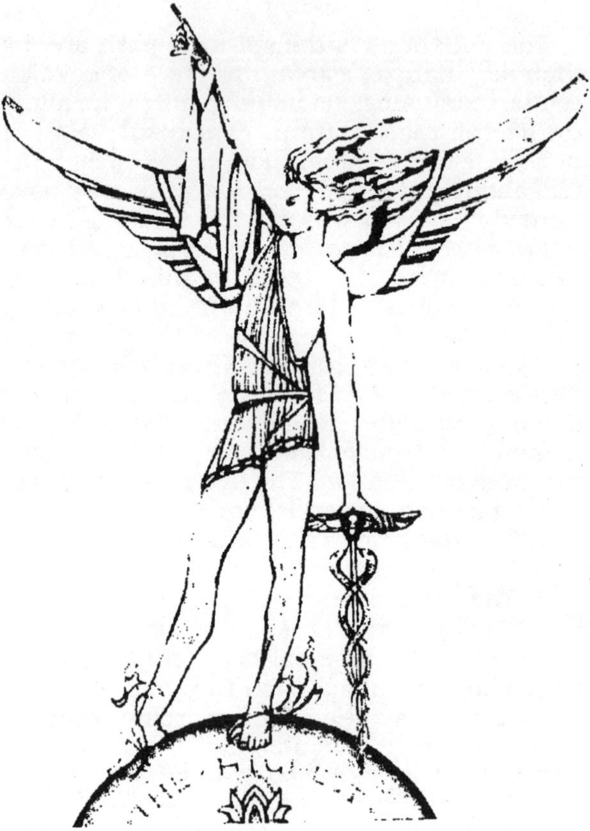

The Brotherhood of Angels and Men
by Geoffrey Hodson

Angels have always been a topic of fascination to men and women, especially those who have embarked on the spiritual path. But most of what has been written about angels has been idle speculation—and outright invention. Some people believe, for example, that human beings become angels after they die. Others would teach us to fear angels, making them into divine accountants who record our sins in preparation for a final and irrevocable judgment.

In point of fact, angels are part of a separate line of evolution—the deva kingdom—which embraces a vast spectrum of consciousness from primitive nature spirits to advanced archangels. Like humans, there are many types of angels. But unlike humans, angels do not incarnate directly through form. Their work and destiny differ from the roles played by men and women.

Despite these differences, men and angels are meant to share the work they do with one another. For many eons, however, this has not been possible; the tendency of mankind to become absorbed in ignorance, selfishness, and negativity has made it impossible for the angel kingdom to draw near. Still, the ideal of a "brotherhood of angels and men" remains active, and it was to promote this ideal that the remarkable book by Geoffrey Hodson, *The Brotherhood of Angels and Men*, was written.

According to Hodson, one of the most gifted

clairvoyants of the 20th century, the text of the book was dictated to him by the angel Bethelda, in the hope of inspiring men and women to learn the true nature of angels and how to communicate effectively with them. Whether written by angel or man, *The Brotherhood of Angels and Men* is a lovely and inspiring book to read. It teaches us not only about angels but also about ourselves, and how to strive for the highest, the noblest, and the best within us and life.

Bethelda begins by describing the purposes served by angels. "Behind every phenomenon you will find a member of our race. Our position in nature is closely akin to that of the engineer; he is not the force himself; he directs it, and as his constant care and oversight are essential to the efficient running of the machine, so the angels, or devas, are essential to the efficient running of the great machine of nature, as well as each individual engine of which it is composed, from atom to archangel."

In specific, seven great divisions of angels are presented:

Angels of power, who direct and release divine energies.

Angels of healing, who seek to aid mankind in healing illness.

Guardian angels of the home, who vivify and protect the noble elements of family life.

Angels who build, embodying archetypal ideas.

Angels of nature, who oversee the distribution of divine forces through nature.

Angels of music, who translate the radiance of God into sound.

Angels of beauty, who preserve and enrich the divine vision.

Because mankind is also interested in these activities, it is reasonable and beneficial for men and women to learn to interact with angels. But striking up a relationship with angelic forces is not the same as building a friendship with another human being. Bethelda is quite insistent that close personal contact with angels should not be the goal of human and angelic interaction. With this injunction clearly stated, he proceeds to describe how a bridge of communication can be established with angels and to suggest a number of invocations which can be used in contacting them.

The angel also describes the proper posture for communicating with angels—and this is the real heart of the book. In nine brilliant chapters, Bethelda touches the essence of excellence, patience, peace, education, joy, vision, thoroughness, unity, and the path. Each of these chapters is a poetic meditation on one of these nine qualities. Swiftly and clearly, we are led to a deeper realization of these archetypes—and, if we read in the right spirit, we learn what it means to commune with the angels.

This is an important book, one which can be read many times over, always renewing our sense of dedication to the divine plan. As Bethelda puts it: "The Angels ask from you, not worship—for that would be inappropriate—but love. The power of our prayers will be enhanced by being offered up with yours; your lives will be enriched by the answer to our common act of praise. Our sphere of usefulness to God will be enlarged by sharing yours; your lives will be enriched, your world made glad, by the inauguration of the Brotherhood of Angels and of Men."

The Sea Priestess
by Dion Fortune

Vivien Le Fay Morgan is a practicing initiate of the Hermetic Path who is able to transform herself into her namesake, Morgan Le Fay, the sea priestess of Atlantis, servant of Isis, and foster daughter of Merlin.

Wilfred Maxwell is an asthmatic young man who falls in love with Morgan and agrees to serve as her priest in a series of magical experiments meant to harness the power of Isis—Isis the Veiled, the Great Mother of Nature, rather than Isis Unveiled, the Heavenly Mother.

What ensues is a magical evocation of the magnetic workings of nature and the orderly intelligence of the planet earth—and how men and women fit into this grand evolutionary scheme. And in the course of exploring and discovering the magnetic relationships of nature, they also explore the relationship between man and woman, male and female, as well as the underlying archetypes of human sexuality.

The Sea Priestess is an amazingly rich novel which stirs the imagination and deepens our appreciation of the power of magic. It is filled with brilliant insights into human psychology—a particular interest of Dion Fortune—and reveals the way in which our character is built up out of the interplay between male and female elements. In the end, however, it becomes the story of why Isis is veiled—and what it means to behold the great Goddess unveiled, in Her supreme glory.

The Sea Priestess is a marvelous novel, a masterpiece of magical fiction.

OM,
The Secret of Ahbor Valley
by Talbot Mundy

Back in the days of British rule in India, an unusual piece of jade happens to come into the hands of the head of the British secret service. Wanting to discover its origin, he assigns Cottswold Ommony, one of his agents, to find out the story of this mysterious jewel.

The pursuit of this jewel leads Ommony on perhaps the greatest mystery of all—the journey into the inner levels of human awareness. For this fist-sized piece of jade has an unusual power to stimulate the mind of the one who gazes into it. In those who are selfish and corrupt, it will reveal the flaws of the dark side of their nature. But in those who are in tune with spirit, it will quicken the higher levels of consciousness.

Ommony's effort to trace the origin of the jade leads him to suspect the motives and acts of a Tibetan lama named Tsiang Samdup. He becomes convinced that Samdup is involved in all manner of nefarious crimes, not the least of which is purchasing young orphaned white girls and transporting them to Ahbor Valley—which is said to be the home of the Masters, but is also known to be a place of great danger. It is said that the natives kill all strangers who enter the district.

Ommony, in fact, has a personal link with Ahbor Valley, because his sister and her husband disappeared there twenty years earlier.

Samdup tours India with a group of actors,

presenting metaphysical plays in one small village after another. Ommony suspects that the theatrical group is a front for what he believes to be Samdup's criminal activities, so he disguises himself as a native Indian actor and joins the cast. He is able to pull off the deception quite successfully, because he is fluent in several Indian languages, although apparently he does not actually fool Samdup.

By being a part of the cast, Ommony also becomes acquainted with Samding, a young protegé of Samdup who plays the role of a venerated Indian saint. The play is about kings and peasants who trade places, believing that it is their roles in life which make them what they are, not their character. But as the play reveals, a good person is good no matter what his place in society, just as a greedy, dishonest person remains selfish. The theme of the play is not always well received, however, as it is a direct attack on the traditional Indian caste system. Performances often lead to riots, and the group is usually forced to leave the village immediately after the play ends.

Suddenly, Samdup leaves the group and departs for an unknown destination. Ommony finds out that Samding is not really a young man, as he had thought, but in fact his own niece, the daughter of his sister and brother-in-law! She was born shortly before her parents died and was saved from death herself by Samdup. More astounding, Samding is in fact the reincarnation of the great saint she has been portraying in the play! Samdup is her teacher.

Ommony could give over his quest at this point, but decides to press on. He traces Samdup into Ahbor Valley, risking both his own life and that of Samdup, who must protect him. The true relationship of Samdup as teacher and Ommony as pupil—soul and personality—comes out into the open, and Samdup instructs Ommony in the ways of the inner life.

Om, The Secret of Ahbor Valley is truly a masterpiece of esoteric fiction and one of Talbot Mundy's greatest novels. It deftly illustrates the true way in which the soul guides and instructs the personality, always leading it but never commanding it. The free will choice of Ommony to pursue the jade and then Samdup is always his own. He is never forced to continue.

The trials and tribulations Ommony encounters—as well as the false suspicions he harbors about Samdup—are likewise powerfully symbolic of the tests of the spiritual path. Mundy writes with a clear understanding of what the life of spirit requires, yet spins his story into an enjoyable, high-spirited, and exciting tale of adventure.

At the end, Samdup shows Ommony the original piece of jade from which the smaller chip was taken—a jewel of such spiritual power that it is studied only by the most advanced spiritual students. And Ommony learns that his niece is to serve as an avatar for modern India, bringing a new message of spirit—a message which surely will be as revolutionary and controversial as the one Jesus brought the Palestinians in His day. Ommony, too, has a role he can play—to serve as his niece's guide.

It is on this note—a note of excitement, revelation, and triumph—that *Om, The Secret of Ahbor Valley*, concludes. It is truly a novel which can lead the reader as well as the hero to a new awareness of the treasure within.

The New Best Seller From
CHUBBS HAGGENDAZ
Eating Your Way To
ENLIGTENMENT
BUTTER
MILK
MILK

In Search of the New Age
by Chris Kilham

One of the most important attributes of the spiritual path is joy. One of the most significant ways we can express joy is through a wholesome sense of humor. Far too many aspirants take the path too seriously. Instead of approaching life as the joyful celebration of divine wisdom and love that it should be, they turn it into some melancholy melodrama in which every cough is a sign of sin and every shred of guilt is deserved.

This is not to imply that we should be flippant about spirit or trivialize the work of light. But it does mean that one of the emerging characteristics of spiritual aspiration should be a healthy sense of humor—especially one that can laugh at itself and at the pitfalls of self-discovery. The illusion of spiritual severity is fed by the fact that few books on the life of spirit, outside of science fiction, treat the subject with humor or levity. There is a virtual black hole when it comes to esoteric humor.

It is therefore gratifying to discover a book that adds a dash of humor to the serious work of illumination. Actually, in the case of *In Search of the New Age*, it is more than a dash—even more than a pinch. It is more like a guru slipping on a banana peel.

The book is a collection of short reviews of the many fads of the so-called "new age." Written by Chris Kilham, it is a marvelous send-up of everything from "dowdy cotton clothing" and "seeing eye dogs for the psychically blind" to "reincarnation life insurance" and crystal enemas that "light up the darkness." The book itself is a loose parody of the whole earth catalogs, a deft combination of pseudo reviews and satirical ads. There are pieces on "Reverend Flung Dung Loon and the Loonies," "I'm OK But You're Not," and "Macroneurotics."

A favorite is "Eating Your Way to Enlightenment," a "review" of a book by Chubbs Haggendaz. As Chubbs explains it, "Some paths require tough, muscular types. But this one is for people who are expanding in all ways."

Another first-rate entry is the "New Age Book List," which features such mythical titles as: *That Was Zen, This is Tao* by La Choy, *The Aquarium Gospel of Jacques the Cousteau* by Levi and Strauss, *The Opening of the Clown Chakra* by Swami Beyondananda, *Here Today, Sodom Gomorrah* by Billy Graham Crackers, *A Knife Thrower's Guide to Acupuncture* by Guy Fat Fang, *There's No Mind, Never Mind—and Zen Some* by Roshi Alzheimer, and *Don't Fall Off a Limb* by Surely Deranged.

There are times when God giggles with joy—and we are meant to giggle with Him. *In Search of the New Age* helps us learn how.

Do-It-Yourself FIREWALKING

So you didn't roast your feet—but you still got burned!

Come on—there's no way in the world it should cost $350 to run across a few hot coals yelling, "cool moss, cool moss." Yet that's exactly what people are paying at firewalks all across the country.

Now, for only $65, you can have your own Do-It-Yourself Firewalking Kit—complete with barbecue, charcoal, lighter fluid, and matches. You supply the positive affirmations, and you're ready to sink your piggies into a searing 1,000-degree pit.

The Do-It-Yourself Firewalking Kit is great for parties and family get-togethers. And you can use it hundreds of times for only a fraction of what it would cost to attend just one high-powered self-improvement seminar.

You'll be the talk of your neighborhood with the Do-It-Yourself Firewalking Kit.

Memories, Dreams, & Reflections
by Carl G. Jung

Dreams and the content of our unconscious minds are subjects of intense interest to many people. In recent years, many books have been written about dreams, but almost all have been disappointing.

The one exception is *Memories, Dreams, & Reflections*, which does not actually purport to be a book about dreams. It is the memoir of the brilliant psychologist Carl G. Jung, written just prior to his death in 1961. Nonetheless, since Jung made a career out of being an intrepid explorer of the subconscious and unconscious, this is a book which teaches us more about dreams than any other book in print.

Jung is absolutely candid in exploring his inner life, even from a very early age. In this way, he shows how his thinking developed—and what it means to lead an examined, intelligent life. He relates his inner life to the outer events which normally fill so much space in an autobiography, but in the case of this book, it is the inner drama that keeps us reading, unable to set the book down, not the outer.

Memories, Dreams, & Reflections is one of the important books of our century. Jung not only summarizes the major discoveries he made in his career in psychology, but also sets a new standard for the intelligent examination of inner phenomena. He makes it clear that the "self" is the only reasonable laboratory for psychological investigation.

The Greater Trumps
by Charles Williams

Good fiction has the opportunity to focus on life in ways that no other form of writing can. It can build a structure of symbols that speak directly to the reader's subconscious; if it is inspired fiction, it can raise this structure of symbols to allegorical or even archetypal levels.

By its nature, good fiction is meant to build suspense, thereby entertaining us. It is therefore the ideal medium for examining the nature of crisis and its power to help us grow—or destroy us. It can be almost poetic and introspective at times, action-oriented at others.

The very best fiction, of course, creates a world of its own, and lures the reader into its mythos. Such novels are animated by the very power of their inspiration—the essence of the author's insight or inspiration.

Every once in a while, a novel is written which seems to be animated by something even greater than the author's imagination. As the story unfolds, it kindles a momentum and sense of drama which carry the reader to a transcendent view of life.

The Greater Trumps by Charles Williams is such a book. It is not an ordinary novel with an esoteric theme; it is as close to an "archetypal experience" as a piece of fiction could be. On the surface, *The Greater Trumps* is a story about the Tarot. The Tarot is a system of symbolism and archetypal design—a system of creative force which holds many keys to the inner patterns of our life. In *The Greater Trumps*, the Tarot comes to life in an unusual way.

Henry, a young man of gypsy descent, and his family have made a study of the Tarot for many years. They have gone so far as to create a set of sculptures of the major Arcana, which they position on a table in an inner sanctum of their home. These Tarot images are almost alive and can be moved in patterns which generate actual changes in physical events.

Lothair Coningsby owns a Tarot deck of unusual power—quite possibly the original Tarot deck from which all others descended. Henry discovers the existence of this deck through Lothair's daughter Nancy, with whom Henry falls in love. Nancy demonstrates an unusual ability to work with the Tarot. Henry determines to steal the magical deck from her father. When his scheme is frustrated, he plots murder, using the forces of the Tarot to manipulate the natural elements, creating a fierce blizzard on Christmas day.

The plot backfires, of course, and both families are threatened by total destruction—and quite possibly the whole human race is in danger, too. But the danger exists only in the minds and hearts of those who misunderstand the true power of life. For Nancy's aunt, Sybil, is a woman of unusual love and wisdom. In one of the most moving conclusions in modern literature, she reveals the unifying principle which holds archetypal forces—and all of creation—together and gives them purpose and direction. She demonstrates the redemptive power of Christ-like love and reaffirms the benevolent nature of life.

Yet neither the plot, as powerful as it is, nor the parallels to the Tarot, as deftly as they are drawn, give *The Greater Trumps* its unique quality. Nor is it Williams' characterizations, which are clearly symbolic—Henry representing the arrogant but well-educated intellect, Nancy representing the intuition, Sybil representing redemptive love, and so on.

No, what sets this novel apart from almost all others is its pace and momentum, which is as strong and as forceful as the blizzard Henry carelessly invokes. Williams carefully weaves together the various elements of his plot, then lets the archetypal power of raw creative force take over and sweep us to the inevitable, perfect conclusion of the book. In chapter after chapter, he gives us brilliant descriptions of the most fundamental conditions of human existence—madness, love, creativity, chaos, self-control, the feminine aspect of life, the masculine force of life, conflict, and the power to triumph over all odds.

In other books, these descriptions would be ponderous, difficult to wade through, but in *The Greater Trumps*, they are the heart of the book. They are filled with the vitality of the story itself and, as the reader finishes each passage, he is tempted to go back and read it again, just to savor it, while impelled to continue reading, to learn what happens next.

We all need to learn the lessons that Henry, Nancy, Sybil, and the other characters of *The Greater Trumps* learn—the lessons of acting, thinking, and feeling in harmony with the rhythms and designs of divine life (to which the Tarot can be a key), not in opposition to them.

The Greater Trumps is an outstanding novel.

Reincarnation
by Leoline L. Wright

The cycles of rebirth constitute one of the most important principles of life, observable not just in nature, the seasons, and the economy, but also in the appearance of human beings in the earth plane. To fully understand the higher self and its methods of manifestation on earth, it is necessary to comprehend the concept of rebirth, or reincarnation.

Unfortunately, it is hard to find intelligent discussions of this subject in print. Reincarnation is a concept that is burdened by glamours and distorted by misconceptions; the vast majority of writings about it are nothing more than fantasies about earlier lifetimes or groundless speculations about the meaning of rebirth.

As a result, Leoline L. Wright's small book, *Reincarnation*, stands out as a refreshing exception to the general rule. Written as part of a series of Theosophical manuals on esoteric principles, it is a clear, concise explanation of the principles of rebirth, what it is that reincarnates, why we do not remember past lives, and how the law of rebirth operates. To quote the text, "The innermost Self of man is a deathless Being, a god, which reclothes itself from age to age in new bodies, that it may undergo all possible experiences in the Universe to which it belongs, and so reach its own most complete growth and self-expression. Rebirth is the pathway of evolution."

As a basic statement of the underlying wisdom of reincarnation, this book is a unique contribution to human understanding.

Life as Carola
by Joan Grant

Carola is the illegitimate daughter of one of the most powerful noblemen in Italy. Yet she and her mother are forced to leave the family castle and wander penniless. They join a band of strolling actors, crisscrossing northern Italy in search of the right opportunity to establish themselves. But opportunity always seems to elude them. Eventually, they break up and Carola enters a convent as a novice.

By this time, she is 18 and has developed many psychic abilities. But the other sisters in the convent do not understand the nature of Carola's gifts. She is accused of witchcraft and forced to undergo torture, until she manages to escape and finds refuge at last.

Like the other novels of Joan Grant, *Life as Carola* is a retelling of a previous life of the author. It is a more difficult life than the one led in *Winged Pharaoh*, but on the whole, it is even more spell-binding. On one level, *Life as Carola* is a fascinating glimpse into life in Italy before the advent of the Renaissance. Through Carola's eyes, we see the beginnings of modern theater, the tremendous extremes between the life of nobility and the common man, and even the awakening of Europe to the existence of the Americas. Yet the real power of this book is its personal account of a very intimate story—the growth of the inner character of a young woman, and her capacity to triumph in even the most adverse situations. This is a book filled with the best qualities of human nature.

Life as Carola is must reading.

The Dragonriders of Pern
by Anne McCaffrey

Every few hundred years, mysterious threads drop on Pern from outer space. If allowed to fall to the ground, they would quickly destroy all vegetation, and Pern would be devastated. There is only one way to fight the threads: the dragons of Pern, guided by their skillful riders, are able to burn the strands before they touch the ground, by belching fire at them.

The skill required to ride the dragons is great, and it separates the riders from the rest of the people of Pern. The riders develop an intense bond with their dragons, and are able to communicate telepathically with them. Eventually, they learn to travel through time as well.

Still, the skills of the dragonriders are not always appreciated—especially since the interval between the threats of the threads is so long. The society of Pern becomes divided between those who champion the dragonriders and those who scorn them.

In *The Dragonriders of Pern*, Anne McCaffrey has created a fascinating world, Pern, in which exciting and deeply symbolic adventures unfold. It is hard to read these three novels—*Dragonflight, Dragonfire,* and *The White Dragon*—without soon seeing the parallels between the dragons and our own subconscious, and between the threads and the thought patterns of mass consciousness which would seek to control us, unless we remain continually vigilant.

There is much fire and drama in these three novels—and plenty of adventure.

Practical Mysticism
by Evelyn Underhill

"The spiritual life is not a special career, involving abstraction from the world of things. It is a part of every man's life; and until he has realised it he is not a complete human being, has not entered into possession of all his powers. It is therefore the function of a practical mysticism to increase, not diminish, the total efficiency, the wisdom and steadfastness, of those who try to practise it."

With these few words, Evelyn Underhill sets the tone for the whole of *Practical Mysticism*, one of the most lucid and helpful explanations of the art of mysticism ever written. Unlike most authors on the subject, Miss Underhill knows exactly what the mystical state is: the art of union with reality. She therefore does not waste any time gushing emotionally about all the wonders of the abstract life, as so many nouveau mystics do; step by step, she shows us what we must do in order to identify with and unite with reality. And at every step, she makes the extra effort to show how mysticism enriches our daily life in practical ways.

Miss Underhill is especially brilliant in her description of contemplation. For far too many people, contemplation is a lazy, reflective state of adoration or devotion. Not so, Miss Underhill explains; true mystical contemplation requires us to stretch beyond our personal capacity and, by an act of will, radiate our adoration or devotion into the whole of creation, transforming it even as we transform ourselves.

Practical Mysticism is a classic in its field.

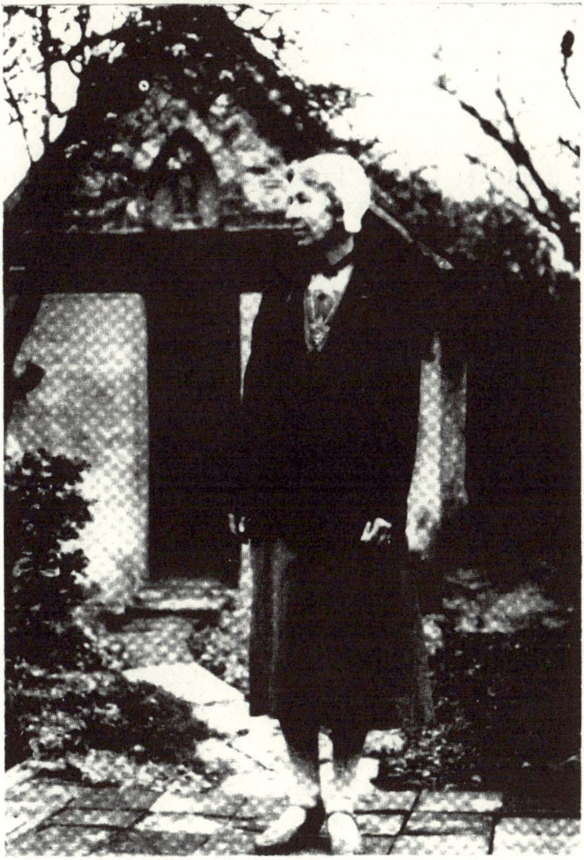

The Chakras
and the Human Energy Fields
by Shafica Karagulla, M.D.
& Dora van Gelder Kunz

One of the newest developments in medicine is what is known as "energy medicine." Scientists working in the fields of homeopathy, acupuncture, magnetic fields, light, and sound now accept the fact that our state of health is influenced by a variety of energies. Learning the proper use of these energies will help us understand the nature of disease, as well as lead us to better techniques for healing the body and personality.

In other words, scientists are beginning to accept what esotericists have known for a long time—that we are multidimensional beings living in a multidimensional universe of invisible energies. These energies not only affect our health but also make up the substance of the mind, emotions, and vital body.

In *The Chakras and the Human Energy Fields*, authors Shafica Karagulla, M.D. and Dora van Gelder Kunz report on their years of study of these energy fields. Dora van Gelder Kunz is an exceptional clairvoyant who is able to see the threefold energy field, or aura, of the human system: the mental, emotional or astral, and the vital or etheric bodies. The late Dr. Karagulla was a medical doctor and psychiatrist who collaborated with Dora for 20 years in this research. Some of the results of their investigations have already been reported in Karagulla's earlier book, *Breakthrough to Creativity*.

Their new book, *The Chakras and the Human Energy Fields*, is based on Dora's clairvoyant investigation of the condition of the human energy fields in a variety of physical and psychological illnesses. All of the case studies were correlated with the medical reports on the subjects, making this study much more relevant and convincing than other reports published recently based on "psychic" observation.

Dora supports the standard esoteric observation that our human state is actually the result of a constant interaction of our mental, emotional, and vital bodies, as well as impacts from the universal fields of energy surrounding each body. The energies involved flow out of, into, and among the force centers or chakras that connect each of these subtle bodies or fields. A careful study of the movement, color, and size of these chakras and the corresponding energy fields can reveal important data about one's psychological and physical health.

This is not the first book on this subject, of course. The growing interest in psychic healing has spawned a number of people who have felt moved to write books on their "clairvoyant" observations of health in general and the chakras in specific.

In most cases, these people have very limited etheric or astral clairvoyance—and virtually no training in correlating what they view psychically with actual disease states. As a result, they have often just reported on one level of chakra activity, as though that was all there was. By missing the threefold field, they have distorted the nature of the chakras and the inner dynamics of health as much as a color-blind artist who can only see grays and greens and therefore paints landscapes in these colors alone. *The Chakras and the Human Energy Fields* rises above this level and consequently distinguishes itself as a volume of clairvoyant research in the tradition of the best of Leadbeater, Besant, and Hodson. It is not just a bunch of casual observations of an opportunist, but the fruit of 20 years of research.

The heart of the book is a series of reports on Dora's observations of patients suffering from cancer, heart disease, strokes, glandular problems, depression, schizophrenia, and addiction. The disturbances in the aura and the disharmony in the customary movement of energy through the chakras that she observed in each case provide major clues to the inner conditions and causes of these illnesses. Dora also reports on the impact on the aura and chakras of taking medication to control anxiety or pain. There is likewise a fascinating description of the inner dimensions of the process of spiritual healing, plus a study of the effects of meditation.

The first part of the book develops a new, more esoteric paradigm about the nature of our human state. The second part reviews basic principles of energy in our subtle bodies and chakras. Parts III and IV deal with Dora's careful clairvoyant observations of the energy fields and chakras in a variety of illnesses and conditions. The final part discusses the role of individual conscious control of healing and the opportunity of using the ideas presented in the book to establish a more holistic view of health.

This is a seminal book which extends our knowledge about the inner side of life and the subtle energies that make up our health—or lead to states of illness.

Return to Elysium
by Joan Grant

Lucina is a Greek girl who grows up in an Utopian enclave, Elysium. As she matures, her natural psychic talents unfold—putting her at odds with Aesculapius, the philosopher and doctor who founded Elysium and is Lucina's guardian.

At first, Aesculapius feigns a scientific interest in Lucina's talents, and suggests that they work together to prove or disprove them. He sets up an experiment designed to trick Lucina, but she uncovers the ruse and passes the test. Aesculapius, unable to accept the facts, reneges on his promise to help Lucina.

Unable to grow further in Elysium, Lucina and two friends sail to Rome, which is just emerging as an empire. There she becomes a priestess in a Delphic temple, dispensing wisdom and healing to any who come. Her reputation grows quickly, but without solid training, success becomes more of a curse than a blessing. At the height of her career, she abandons it to run away with her lover, a Roman senator.

Return to Elysium is a delightful book to read, filled with insights into human nature. It portrays the conflict between science and intuition—and also provides us with a profound description of the power of self-deception, buttressed by solely intellectual assumptions, to prevent us from understanding ourself and our destiny. It also features one of the most intriguing endings in all of modern literature.

This is first-rate esoteric fiction.

The Betty Book
by Stewart Edward White

If one were to draw up a list of the 25 most important classics in the field of spiritual growth and the inner life, *The Betty Book* would probably be somewhere in the top 10. Amid all the current hubbub about "channeling," it is sometimes easy to forget that some of the best books on the inner life and our exploration of it were written 50 years ago—or more.

The Betty Book stands in a class by itself. First published in 1937, it chronicles more than 20 years of mediumistic exploration conducted by Stewart White through the mediumship of his wife Betty. What makes *The Betty Book* so outstanding, though, is that it is not just the usual collection of evidential communications with "dead" mothers and aunts. It is a carefully reasoned, lucid exploration of the inner side of our being and what it means to "grow in spirit."

Betty is helped in this work by the "Invisibles," a group of discarnates who take turns speaking through Betty or leading her through an experiment or experience which she then reports back to Stewart. As such, the quality of mediumship and discovery in this book (and subsequent ones written by Stewart) is much higher and more refined than in the usual books on channeling or mediumship. Beyond that, the insights into human life are fascinating and compelling. They make sense—and challenge us to rethink our assumptions. *The Betty Book* introduces us to the grandest journey of all—the discovery of our own inner self.

The Arthurian Saga
by Mary Stewart

The legend of King Arthur and his magician Merlin has been popular in every age. Each generation produces new versions of this romantic tale, for the themes of the lives of Arthur and Merlin are as fascinating and informative as they are timeless. Mary Stewart's four-book set on Arthur and Merlin conveys fresh insight into the meaning of these heroes to our culture. It begins with *The Crystal Cave*, continues with *The Hollow Hills* and *The Last Enchantment*, and reaches its conclusion in *The Wicked Day*.

At first, the stories focus on Merlin, from the turmoil of his childhood through his training to be a magician to the fulfillment of his destiny. In this sense, these books are the story of a man who slowly comes to understand his affinity to magical forces and how God chooses to use him to aid his king. Those who have felt drawn by higher forces beyond their control will be able to identify with these elements of Merlin's life.

Merlin, of course, foretells the rise and fall of Arthur, and fate, destiny, and prophecy are powerful themes coursing through all four books. Gradually, however, the emphasis shifts from the magical to the human, until in *The Wicked Day*, Arthur learns the full meaning of his destiny: "We have let ourselves be blinded by prophecy. We have lived under the edge of doom....But fate is made by men, not gods. Our own follies, not the gods, foredoom us. The gods are spirits; they work by men's hands, and there are men brave enough to stand up and say: I am a man; I will not."

The Nine Billion Names of God
by Arthur C. Clarke

Arthur Clarke's great knack as a writer of science fiction is his ability to weave what he calls the "wide view" of life into entertaining stories. Clarke has a firm understanding of how the evolutionary impulse of life challenges, pushes, cajoles, and bullies us to grow, in spite of ourselves, and sooner or later, this theme pops up in almost everything he writes.

This is certainly the case in *The Nine Billion Names of God*, a collection of Clarke's 25 favorite short stories among the more than 100 that he has written. From the title story, which flirts deliciously with the creative power of the Word, to the startling, rudely awakening finale of "The Star," these stories expand the scope of our own thinking, about ourselves and about life in general. In its own way, each story challenges preconceived notions and cultural prejudices which tend to keep us from discovering the wider meanings and implications of life.

Yet each story is fresh and original, not just another bucket drawn from the same well. Clarke has amazing dexterity, making us believe he is a mystery writer in "Trouble with Time," the story of an inept art thief on Mars; a humorist in "The Reluctant Orchid," in which the purpose of nurturing love is forgotten, then recovered; and a prophet in "The Sentinel," which became the basis for the film *2001: A Space Odyssey*.

These stories are real gems.

After We Die, What Then?
by George W. Meek

Few subjects are more important—and more commonly ignored—than just what happens to us following death. Theology has tried to answer the question, but has done little but stir up fear and guilt. Science has also tried to guide us, but has done even worse, succeeding only in planting seeds of doubt.

George W. Meek is an engineer who has led the effort to discover just exactly what does happen after we die. Meek first collected his findings in a book published eight years ago. But he did not stop his research—or his discoveries. So, a new and freshly revised edition was in order.

After We Die, What Then? is possibly the most comprehensive book on the nature of life after death in print today. The book is divided into four parts. In the first, Meek presents an overview of the subject and why it is reasonable to expect life to continue.

In the second, he examines the plentiful evidence for survival, from spirit photographs and mediumistic records to near-death memories. This section is followed by a chapter in which Meek answers 50 of the common questions about death.

While some of this material has been updated, the bulk of Meek's new material in this edition is presented in the final section, in which he reports on successful experiments to speak with spirits by radio-like electronic devices.

This book establishes the continuity of life as fact, not speculation.

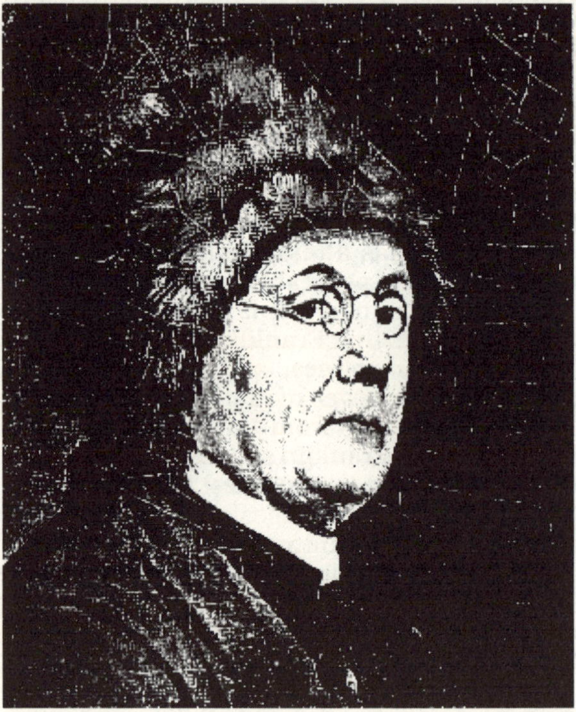

Fart Proudly
by Benjamin Franklin

Benjamin Franklin was one of the greatest thinkers this country ever produced. As a writer and printer, he played an important role in shaping the American perspective on life.

Unfortunately, the picture we get of Franklin from our traditional schooling is not at all like the real person. There was a bawdy, scurrilous dimension to Franklin's character that was all too eager to ignite the flames of controversy—and keep them burning.

Fart Proudly is a testament to the satirical rogue that lived peaceably inside the philosopher and statesman. It is a collection of the funniest pieces that Franklin wrote during his lengthy career—pieces, as the subtitle indicates, that you never read in school.

The title derives from the first item in the book, in which Franklin suggests that a scientific society conduct a contest to find a pill or perfume which, when ingested, would turn the odors of flatulence into pleasing aromas.

Other pieces included in the collection are "On Choosing a Mistress," "Rules on Making Oneself Disagreeable," "The Grand Leap of the Whale," and "The Court of the Popular Press."

The collection was compiled and edited by Carl Japikse, who also added an introduction and an afterword, in which Dr. Franklin appears in a dream and comments on the loss of freedom in this country during the past 200 years.

Everyone striving to think clearly will enjoy this small book immensely.

The Powers of Thought
by Mikhael Aïvanhov

Mikhael Aïvanhov was born and raised in Bulgaria. In 1937, his teacher sent him to France to escape the eventual threat of communism. In France, Aïvanhov began his teaching.

Aïvanhov did not write any books during his lifetime, but his many lectures and talks were recorded by his students. Since his death in 1986, his followers have been working to collect these many talks thematically into books.

The Powers of Thought is one of the most intriguing and important of these books. Aïvanhov expresses himself lucidly and powerfully as he explores the hidden nature of thought (and, to some degree, emotion) and teaches us how important it is to discipline our thoughts and tap their creative potential. He is especially eloquent on the topic of psychic pollution:

"Everybody thinks; the only question is how they think. Go and stir up a heap of manure and you will smell a nauseating stench. Well, often enough, that is how people think: they stir up piles of manure and it stinks!"

Or again: "Thought is a force, a power, an instrument given to man by God, so that he, too, may be a creator in the same way that God is a creator: in beauty and perfection. By means of his thought, man can make contact with all kinds of different substances, quintessences and creatures in either the divine or the infernal regions, and if he does not know that thought is creative, he may easily get involved in such negative, disintegrating preoccupations that he destroys himself."

Aïvanhov proceeds to make it abundantly clear how ignorant people foolishly use the power of thought to destroy themselves. He correctly points out that thoughts are living beings which, like humans and other animals, strive to live as long as they can.

"Some thoughts have a very short life, whereas others can survive for hundreds and even thousands of years. Yes, there are still thoughts abroad in the world today that have been there since the days of ancient Egypt, Syria, or Chaldea, or even Atlantis. Some of these thoughts are so evil and venomous that they are still destructive, whereas others, on the contrary, are still the source of great blessings."

Depending upon the quality of our consciousness, we will either be dominated and exploited by such thoughts as pessimism—or we will be served and inspired by such thoughts as gratitude and joy. The key to human and spiritual growth, he argues, lies in our capacity for discernment—to discriminate between healthy, wholesome thoughts which emanate from spirit, on the one hand, and evil, materialistic thoughts that have arisen from greed and selfishness, on the other hand.

Having laid this foundation, Aïvanhov then proceeds to discuss how thoughts materialize on the physical plane—and how we can learn to use them creatively and spiritually to improve conditions on earth.

Aïvanhov quickly dispatches the simplistic notion of positive thinking so popular with spiritual novices. "If you want to get a lump of sugar to jump out of the sugar bowl into your mouth, you can concentrate for all you are worth, but it won't happen, and you will be discouraged and disappointed. Whereas, all you have to do is stretch out your hand, pick up a lump of sugar and pop it into your mouth: no fuss or bother! Nature gave you a hand which you can use to pick things up. You will say, 'But what can you do with thought, then?' With thought you can do far more important things than that, but you must know its nature and its mechanism; you must know how it works."

Toward that end, Aïvanhov spends the rest of the book detailing the nature and mechanism of thought—and advocating meditation and prayer as the ideal activities for training the mind to think at full potential. He patiently demonstrates what it means to build constructive bridges between the plane of thought and the physical plane, so that we can harness this enormous power safely and constructively.

One of his most inspired chapters is on "The Strength of Spirit," in which he clearly states that true thinking emanates from spirit and infuses all that we do with the light of spirit. "The essential, the only thing that counts, is life, the spirit. What is the point of pursuing non-essentials? It would be true to say that the real difference between an Initiate and an ordinary person is precisely this: the Initiate is only concerned with what is essential."

The Powers of Thought is an essential guide.

Atlas Shrugged
by Ayn Rand

First published in 1957, this great novel by Ayn Rand is still relevant today, as it clearly highlights the basic themes of the Spirit of America and the triumph of the creative individual over the parasitic forces of inertia.

Atlas Shrugged is set in a society which has gone sour through its surrender to elements that champion mediocrity, decry elitism, fear excellence, and are committed to a program of economic cannibalism which slowly destroys the productive elements of society in order to support the tyranny of the masses.

Its heroes are a small group of people who still possess the creative spirit of initiative and self-sufficiency on which America was founded, and cherish the freedoms which make the independence of the individual possible. As the destruction of the fabric of society proceeds, these productive individuals are accused of selfishness, greed, and social irresponsibility. Actually, their only crimes are good sense and an enlightened work ethic.

Finally, they decide they are no longer willing to carry on their backs the hoards of welfare consumers. So they retreat to a secret valley and begin a new society, which fosters genius, initiative, self-sufficiency, and cooperation.

Atlas, of course, is the Greek Titan who carries the world on his shoulders. He is symbolic of the creative and productive elements of society, which truly support the world. In this great novel, Atlas finally shrugs off his parasitic burden and achieves freedom.

Esoteric Christianity
by Annie Besant

There are two sides to every major religion—the familiar teachings and creeds the average person associates with the religion, and the inner or esoteric teachings which are the religion's link to the Ancient Wisdom. The familiar teachings of a religion are easily found—in its dogma, its scripture, the life story of its founder, and the writings of its saints or great teachers. The esoteric tradition is usually not so easily found. It is the record of what the visionaries of the religion, from the founder to the present day, have discovered about spirit. Often, it is not even known to most of the religion's priests, having been preserved only in the writings of mystics or passed on orally.

The esoteric side of Christianity certainly fits this pattern. It flourished for the first several centuries after Christ and made a rich contribution to early Christian thought. Its primary guardians at that time were the early Gnostics. But as time passed, dissension within the ranks of the Gnostics betrayed their rich treasure, and political pressures within the Church of Rome forced it underground.

Nevertheless, the inner side of Christianity has survived, carried on by the inspired mystics, saints, and occultists of every century. Indeed, no matter how hard the official church may try to purge these teachings, they will always survive, because they are nothing less than the actual roots of Christianity in the infinite love and wisdom of God. Any enlightened person who studies Christianity "rediscovers" its esoteric side and brings it to our attention again. The flame of truth never dies, even though its outer light may be obscured from time to time.

Annie Besant is clearly one who is attuned to the rich esoteric tradition of Christianity. Her book, *Esoteric Christianity*, is a remarkable exploration of early Christian teachings, how they have been preserved throughout the ages, and their relevance to our lives today.

Mrs. Besant was an early Theosophist. She followed H.P. Blavatsky as president of the Theosophical Society and collaborated with C.W. Leadbeater on a number of books—as well as writing a good many books on her own. *Esoteric Christianity* is one of the best, remaining, even after all these years, a much-needed supplement to the historical record of Christianity. Her search through the surviving writings of early Christian scholars and Gnostics reveals that their insights into the true message of the Christ were both brilliant and pertinent to daily life. She gives us an invaluable glimpse into the practice of Christianity before it became deadened by dogma and arthritic with tradition.

In the early days of Christianity, the central role of intuition to the life of spirit was understood. The spiritual gifts Paul described were more common and prized. The fact of reincarnation was accepted and a knowledge of the inner planes was considered important to the conduct of a spiritual life on earth. The role of initiation in spiritual growth was respected. Angels were not something that showed up at the birth of Christ and then no more—the value of invoking these forces was appreciated.

Mrs. Besant begins with a brief examination

of how this esoteric tradition began, what it taught, and how it was "lost." She then turns her attention to a thorough exploration of what she deems the primary themes of esoteric Christianity, relating the story of the historical Christ with the inner teachings of the mythic and mystic Christ, probing the inner meaning of atonement, resurrection, ascension, and the trinity, and concluding with an evaluation of the esoteric value of prayer, forgiveness of sins, the major sacraments, and Christian revelation.

Esoteric Christianity is a major book. The mere fact it could be written is proof the wisdom of God never dies. No matter how many books are burned, or how much political intrigue sabotages religious teachings, nor how many Inquisitions are conducted, the true spirit of religion cannot be surpressed. It will be carried on, and is always available to esoteric students.

It is also an exciting book to read, at least for anyone interested in the inner life of Christianity. Where familiar teachings and dogma fall short, never quite satisfying the enlightened quest for understanding, Mrs. Besant's story of the early teachings clarifies much of what has been obscure and incomplete. It is highly recommended.

The Fullness of Human Experience
by Dane Rudhyar

Dane Rudhyar, who died in 1985 at the age of 90, was one of the clearest thinkers and writers of our age. We have long wanted to feature one of his books, yet many of the most readily available are highly specialized. It is therefore with pleasure that we recommend his final book, *The Fullness of Human Experience.*

This new book is a fitting climax to Rudhyar's extensive body of writings, as it takes many of the essential themes he dealt with throughout his life and focuses them in one ultimate investigation—an investigation into the meaning and purpose of human life and individuality, from which he draws conclusions as to what values, practices, and pursuits lead to the "fullness" of human activity.

Rudhyar begins by restating his basic concept of wholeness and the experience of periodic change, showing how the individual fits into the larger whole, draws his meaning from it, and must be interpreted within a holistic context. He goes on to point out that certain rhythms of change govern both the whole and the individual, generating opportunity, problems, challenges, crises, and growth. Somewhere on the road between fatalistic superstition and existential nonsense, the human mind begins to sense these rhythms and learns to cooperate with them, inducing growth.

The Fullness of Human Experience is the crowning achievement of a mature mind.

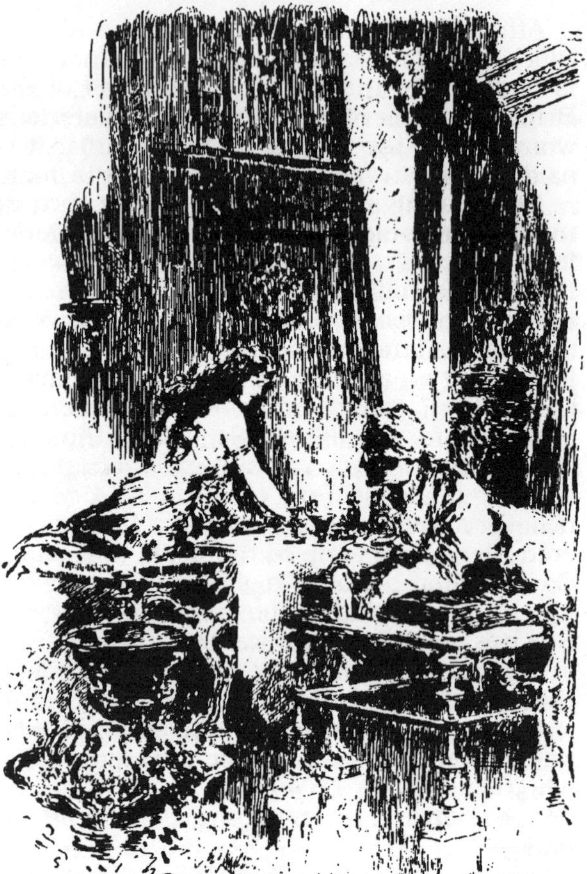

King—of the Khyber Rifles
by Talbot Mundy

Athelstan King is an officer in the Khyber Rifles, a British regiment stationed in India. He is also one of the primary operatives of the British secret service. Yasmini is a mysterious woman from the hills of northern India. It is said that whatever she commands, it is done.

King is assigned to locate the source and put to an end a rumored uprising among the Moslems in the hills. He is told that he will be working with Yasmini, who has been recruited for the same purpose. Just catching up with Yasmini is assignment enough, however, as she leads King on a merry chase into the heart of the Khyber Pass and beyond—to Khinjan Caves, a hideout for the hill people. Along the way, King discovers that Yasmini may actually be working for herself, not the British. A devout believer in reincarnation, Yasmini has discovered an ancient tomb in the heart of Khinjan Caves—a tomb that tells of triumph and glory by a man and a woman thousands of years ago. She has arrived at the belief that she and King are the reincarnated lovers, and devises a plan that will enable them to conquer the world.

But for all of Yasmini's hypnotic and telepathic powers, she is unable to seduce King, who turns her own plan against her and uses her position and power to thwart the imminent *jihad.*

King—of the Khyber Rifles is a thrilling story in the true Talbot Mundy tradition. It is also a marvelous study in the interactions of the male and female aspects of duality.

The Twelve Powers of Man
by Charles Fillmore

Charles Fillmore was one of the founders of the Unity Church. During his career, he wrote many books. Perhaps the most useful and universal is *The Twelve Powers of Man*.

Fillmore bases his book on the Biblical reference of Jesus telling His followers that they shall sit with Him on the twelve thrones, judging the twelve tribes of Israel. The "thrones," according to Fillmore are the primary faculties of mankind; the "tribes" are the spiritual qualities we need to develop in order to release the power of spirit within us.

Fillmore defines the twelve powers as faith, strength, wisdom, love, mastery, the imagination, understanding, will, order, enthusiasm, renunciation, and the life essence. To each of these powers he devotes a whole chapter, showing the role this power plays in our human consciousness, how we tend to misuse it, and what it means to redeem our use of this divine force.

This is not just another collection of metaphysical platitudes, however. Fillmore writes with a rare level of insight and wisdom. He makes it clear from the beginning that he is not talking about the ordinary applications of these powers in human life, but rather the subtle forces which operate at subconscious and superconscious levels. In a very real sense, he is describing the esoteric basis for the processes of transformation and transfiguration.

The Twelve Powers of Man is a powerful book, indeed.

Moon Magic
by Dion Fortune

*"The moon is riding high and clear,
O Lovely one, draw near, draw near;
To lonely men on lonely ways
Come down in dream of silver haze.
Persephone, Persephone,
All in the end shall come to thee."*

The sequel to *The Sea Priestess*, in which Dion Fortune introduced the character of Vivien Le Fay Morgan or Lilith Le Fay, *Moon Magic* is a haunting, powerful novel, one of a kind. For it is written through the persona of Lilith herself, who claims to be a priestess of the goddess Isis—the divine feminine principle.

As such, this novel boldly explores the archetypal forces of manhood, womanhood, and sexuality, and unveils the inner levels of magic which work through them in the great drama of creativity. *Moon Magic* does not hesitate to shake worn-out customs and rituals until they are exposed, but it does a great deal more than shock. It is a finely tuned novel, which leads us step by step to a truer awareness of what is involved in establishing a profound intuitive rapport with the inner forces and dimensions of life.

The symbol of the moon, of course, is an ancient one for the feminine principle and its unique capacity to unleash the full potency of the masculine principle and produce union— between two lovers, the personality and the soul, and humanity and the divine.

In the final analysis, *Moon Magic* is a mystery novel—a novel which explores the mystery of who we are in a thoroughly captivating way.

The Light Within Us
by Carl Japikse

There are many people who are sincerely devoted to growing spiritually and becoming more attuned to their higher selves, yet do not make much progress. They try this method and that technique, but exhaust themselves in a series of false starts. They have enough devotion. What they lack is *understanding*—knowledge of how to tread the spiritual path.

The Light Within Us provides this special knowledge. It is a step-by-step guide to spiritual growth which is written to help aspirants of all backgrounds understand what spirit is, what it means to grow spiritually, and how to do it. Written by Carl Japikse, it is a lucid and easy-to-grasp presentation of the timeless knowledge of who we are and why we are here.

The instructions which form the core of the text are a modern, updated translation of an ancient text on raja yoga written thousands of years ago by a teacher named Patanjali. Japikse has taken this basic text, transcribed it into contemporary English, and added his own penetrating insights into spiritual growth.

The result is a profound examination of the spiritual path. The text is split into four parts. The first examines the nature of consciousness. The second describes the process of integration. The third explores creative mastery. The fourth is entitled, "The Light of the World."

The Light Within Us is a guide for all who truly want to grow and discover their heritage of light.

It is highly recommended.

Visible Light
by C.J. Cherryh

"A story is a moment of profound examination of things in greater reality and sharper focus than we usually see them." With this statement, C.J. Cherryh introduces the short stories in *Visible Light*, all of which take us beyond our ordinary perspectives.

In "Casandra," for instance, we are taken inside the personality of a clairvoyant who must live with a continual and maddening awareness of the disastrous future of those about her. It reminds us that too much attention given to our future, good or bad, can so frustrate us that we spoil our current opportunities.

"Threads of Time" is a tale about the time police, who work to stop those who would tamper with the present by changing the past. The story vividly teaches us how easily opportunities are lost—and difficulties created.

The story "Companions" concerns a marooned spaceman and his robot aide. In it, we learn about the many facets of the human mind, as the hero confronts himself in his loneliness. In the process, we learn how our concrete thinking can imprison and destroy our spiritual dimensions.

Cherryh says we tend to systematize what we see and then see what we want, and thereby end up making fools of ourselves. To stop this tendency, we must learn to penetrate our assumptions and habits and see things as they are. The stories in *Visible Light* are all mind stretchers guaranteed to make us more thoughtful and perceptive.

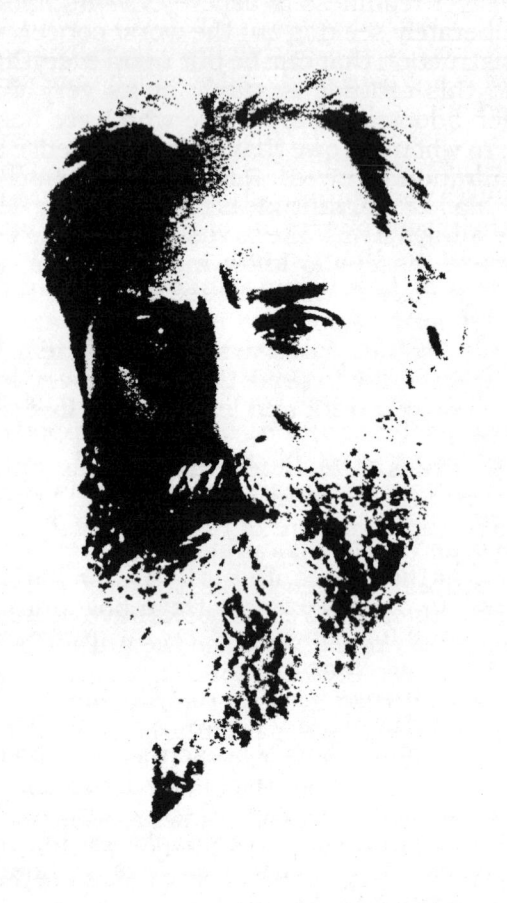

The Inner Life
by C. W. Leadbeater

"One of the worst features of modern life is its eager readiness to believe evil—its habit of deliberately seeking out the worst conceivable construction that can be put upon everything. And this attitude is surely at its very worst when adopted toward those who have helped us, to whom we owe thanks for knowledge and inspiration received. Remember the words of the Master: 'Ingratitude is not one of our vices.' It is always a mistake to rush madly into criticism of those who know more than we; it is more seemly to wait and see what the future brings forth. Apply the test of time and the result; 'by their fruits ye shall know them.' Let us make a rule to think the best of every man; let us do our work and leave others free to do theirs."

So writes C.W. Leadbeater on the topic of criticism in *The Inner Life*, one of the greatest books on the nature of the inner planes and spiritual growth ever written.

Leadbeater received his share of criticism during his career. Yet his books have withstood the test of time. If we judge the author by the fruit he bore, C.W. Leadbeater is surely one of the outstanding lights of the new age.

The Inner Life is particularly profound because Leadbeater was one of the greatest clairvoyants of his time. His clairvoyance was not just limited to astral phenomena, as is usually the case, but extended to the mental plane. The depth and clarity of his observations are therefore in a class by themselves.

This is important, because we do not have many reliable guides to the inner life. Some religious and mystical writings do provide us with clues and descriptions but, unfortunately, far too many religious writings end up presenting a very narrow view of life.

Mediums have given us another source of commentary on the nature of the inner life, but in all too many cases these descriptions are unreliable. The great weakness of mediumship (and the fad phenomenon of channeling) is that it is so easily colored by the subconscious expectations of the medium.

As a result, it is common to hear people—even in metaphysics—simply state, when asked about the inner life: "Nobody knows." This uncertainty is then countered by the rigidity of fundamentalism—that we do not need to know, just *believe.*

Well, C.W. Leadbeater *did* know, and *The Inner Life* is a lucid, articulate, and thorough description of what he knew about the spiritual dimensions of life. The book is a collection of lectures and talks the Bishop delivered to students at the headquarters of the Theosophical Society in Adyar, India, during the summer of 1910. These talks have been edited and arranged by subject into a comprehensive tour of the inner life. The contents include:
- The Great Ones and the way to them.
- Religion.
- The Theosophical attitude.
- The higher planes.
- The Ego and his vehicles.
- The after-death life.
- Astral work.
- The mental body and the power of thought.

- Psychic faculties.
- Devas and nature spirits.
- Reincarnation.
- Karma.

Leadbeater's comments on each of these topics are based on his own direct observation of the way life is, not just physically, but at its inner dimensions as well. In talking about criticism and prejudice, for instance, the Bishop proceeds to state that these conditions are like diseases of the mind. In fact, he becomes quite specific:

"If a prejudice should grow up in the man, thought on that particular subject ceases altogether, and a small eddy forms in which the mental matter runs round and round until it coagulates and becomes a kind of wart....This foul thickened mass blocks all free movement either outward or inward; it prevents him on the one hand from seeing accurately...and on the other from sending out any clear thought.

"These diseased spots in the mental body are unfortunately also centers of infection; the inability to see clearly increases and spreads.... Religious prejudice...completely prevents any approach to rational thought with regard to the subject. Unfortunately, a very large number of people have the whole of that part of their mental bodies which should be occupied with religious matters inactive, ossified and covered with warts, so that even the most rudimentary conception of what religion really is remains utterly impossible for them."

This kind of brilliant description of the true nature of the life within us makes *The Inner Life* one of the most valuable books of its kind. It should be part of the library of every student.

Waldo & Magic, Inc.
by Robert Heinlein

Waldo & Magic, Inc. is a double treat, in that it is really two novellas in a single book, both vintage Heinlein and brimming with esoteric significance.

Waldo is the story of a great genius who lives in the isolation of outer space, apart from mankind, which he holds in contempt. But humanity is faced with an energy crisis strangely paralleling a personal affliction Waldo has had since birth—myasthenia gravis. Waldo has no choice but to return to earth, where he unlocks the secret of unlimited energy while discovering his own tie with humanity, thereby curing himself. The accuracy with which Heinlein portrays the nature of energy is amazing. Few novels are more brilliantly conceived and executed than this one—or more satisfying to read.

Magic, Inc. is a different kind of tale—a major confrontation between the forces of white magic and black magic for control of the government—and through it, the practice of all magic. The confrontation leads the heroes of the story into the "Half World" for the final showdown—in which, of course, light does triumph over darkness. The action in the "Half World" is a remarkable revelation of the way things actually occur in some dimensions of the astral plane, and what it requires to interact with it safely. As with all Heinlein stories, there is a serious message behind all of the great, good fun and excitement of the actual story.

The two novellas of *Waldo & Magic, Inc.* represent esoteric fiction at its best.

The Seven Human Temperaments
by Geoffrey Hodson

One of the most fascinating new teachings to emerge in the last 100 years has been the concept of the seven rays—that there are seven divine energies which are the creative builders of all of life. Out of these seven rays, in an almost infinite number of combinations, everything that is has been created. An understanding of these rays, therefore, and how they act at the inner levels of life to produce changes and growth at the outer levels, provides enormous insight into just about every facet of life.

The workings of the rays, however, is a complex subject; many contemporary authors have made a muddle of them, misconstruing their true esoteric meaning. As fascinating as the subject is, therefore, we should take care to study it with discernment.

Beyond any doubt, the best introduction to the rays currently in print is *The Seven Human Temperaments* by Geoffrey Hodson. Hodson, an outstanding clairvoyant, limits his treatment of the rays to their influence on humanity, yet nonetheless presents a very readable discussion of each ray, its ideal, and some of the ways people behave under its influence. He also provides a chart which makes it easy to study similarities and differences among the rays.

Far more work will be done on the importance of the rays in the future. But for a good, solid foundation in the subject, *The Seven Human Temperaments* is the place to begin.

Edgar Cayce's Story of Attitudes & Emotions
by Jeffrey Furst

Edgar Cayce is the best-known psychic America has yet produced, and his work is a veritable treasure of esoteric insights. Over a span of 40 years he gave some 15,000 psychic readings, all of which have been carefully preserved.

One of the areas in which the Cayce readings are the most profound is in their commentary on the roots of our emotional problems, their relation to physical illness, and the power we have to redirect and enlighten our attitudes. Author Jeffrey Furst has researched the Cayce readings dealing with emotional problems and their cures, drawn them together, and added commentary of his own to tie it all together.

The result is *Edgar Cayce's Story of Attitudes and Emotions*, a thoroughly readable and very helpful examination of emotions, ethics, feelings, and morality. It pulls no punches in describing the true effect of negative emotions such as fear, anger, envy, and depression on ourselves and others, or in describing how gossip, criticism, and selfishness damage our subtle bodies—our psychological mechanism.

At the same time, it makes clear the value of cultivating wholesome emotions such as goodwill, tolerance, cheerfulness, calmness, and compassion.

We all have much to learn about our use of the emotions. *Edgar Cayce's Story of Attitudes and Emotions* makes an excellent workbook for personal growth.

Great Lion of God
by Taylor Caldwell

"Many novels and books about St. Paul have told in marvelous detail what he *did* and accomplished in his life and missionary journeys. I am concerned with what he *was*, a man like ourselves with our own despairs, doubts, anxieties and angers and intolerances, and 'lusts of the flesh.' Many books have been concerned with the Apostle. I am concerned with the man, the human being, as well as the dauntless saint."

So writes Taylor Caldwell in the introduction to her historical novel, *Great Lion of God*, a fictionalized account of the life of St. Paul. What follows the introduction is a masterful fulfillment of her goal.

It is really the story of struggle. Paul was born into a wealthy Jewish family and educated as a Pharisee. To pursue a closer relationship with God, and service to the Christ, he cut himself off from the support of his family, his friends, his wealth, and his religion. He estranged himself from the life of earth to know the life of heaven, and reveal it to others.

Yet none of these sacrifices came easily. Paul was a sensitive person, torn between the pairs of opposites that every spiritual aspirant must face. He knew well his human weaknesses—but valued even more the love of God.

Taylor Caldwell is brilliant at getting inside the thoughts and feelings, the values and motivations of her characters. *Great Lion of God* is not just a story of Paul; it is the story of everyone who struggles to become a servant of God.

Odin, on the World Tree, sees the Runes

The Book of Runes
by Ralph Blum

The struggle to relate to the sublime and invisible nature of life is an eternal one for all spiritual aspirants. There are many principles and guidelines which can direct us in this quest, but, unfortunately, we have few "road maps" which can provide *specific* advice about our unique situation and our next step on our spiritual journey.

The Book of Runes is one of the few road maps available to us. It can help us explore our inner life and point out constructive possibilities for action. Like the Tarot and the I Ching, the Runes employ a system of archetypal symbols through which we can tap the wisdom and order of our inner life. By consulting them, we can enrich our understanding of our creative possibilities and how we may be blocking progress.

The Runes are an ancient system of divination whose origin can be traced back to the Germanic tribes of northern Europe. They were last in current use in Iceland during the late Middle Ages. In their time, they served as the I Ching of the Vikings.

The Book of Runes is actually a three-in-one combination: a set of 25 small stones, a bag to hold them, and a small hardbound book by Ralph Blum. In the book, Blum describes the history of the Runes, how to consult them, and how to interpret each of the stones. The stones themselves are thumb-sized, flat pieces of fired clay with a glyph representing the Rune on one side. The opposite side is blank.

Blum has succeeded in reviving an otherwise-lost system of divination. And he has done so in a refreshing way. Rather than just translating some old text, Blum investigated the Runes *intuitively*, combining his own research with frequent consultations of the I Ching and observation of signs and omens.

As Blum states, the motto of the Runes could be the same as the words carved at the gate of the Oracle at Delphi: *know thyself.* By consulting the Runes, we are put in contact with our inner guidance. The Runes can become, therefore, an oracle, teacher, and friend.

"Consulting the Runes enables us to bypass the strictures of reason, the fetters of conditioning and the momentum of habit. For a brief span of interacting with the Runes you are declaring a free zone in which your life is malleable, vulnerable, open to transformation," writes Blum. In this way, working with the Runes can open a doorway to the exploration of our higher self and our personal Odyssey.

As with the I Ching and the Tarot, simple questions which can be answered "yes" or "no" are not the best to use. It is the issue which must be defined, then explored.

One way to test a tool of divination is to ask it about itself. We consulted the Runes with this issue: "What is the best way to use the Runes?" We used a three-stone layout in which the first stone represents the situation as it is; the second the course of action called for; and the third the new situation to evolve.

The response was quite illuminating. For the situation as it is, *Laguz* came up. In reading Blum's commentary, certain phrases seemed to leap out: "This Rune...signals a time for cleansing, for revaluing, reorganizing, realigning...you may be called to study spiritual matters in readiness for self-transformation." In other words, the Runes are an excellent guide to self-discovery and growth.

The second stone, *Sowelu*, described the course of action called for: "This Rune...embodies the impulse toward self-realization and indicates the path you must follow...you must become conscious of your essence—your personal myth—and bring it into form."

The new situation that would evolve was depicted in the third stone, *Wunjo:* "This Rune is a fruit-bearing branch....Now you can freely receive blessings....There is a new clarity which may call for you to renounce existing plans, ambitions, goals."

The Runes, quite obviously, are telling us that they are best used to tap into our inner wisdom—the plans and designs of our soul—so that we can use its guidance and power to transform our thinking and action. As Blum summarizes it, "Rune casting is high adventure....As we start to make contact with our Knowing Selves, we will begin to hear messages of profound beauty and true usefulness."

The Real World of Fairies
by Dora van Gelder

Confined by our senses to the physical world, as most of us are, there is much about the inner dimensions of life which escapes our observation and understanding. And yet, our confinement is mostly voluntary. There are many ways out of it.

One of the most delightful is to spend an afternoon or evening reading *The Real World of Fairies*, a book as charming as the creatures it describes. Dora van Gelder is a gifted clairvoyant who has had a strong rapport with the fairy kingdom since her childhood in Java. Through her personal observations and experiences, we are led into an inner dimension which is everywhere around us, but unknown to the vast majority of humans.

Fairies are creatures of light and motion, a part of the angelic kingdom. They work directly with the forces of nature—fire, earth, air, and water—in supporting and tending the development of life in this marvelous garden, Earth.

In this book, Miss van Gelder describes the various kinds of fairies and their levels of evolution, but she does much more as well. She captures the spirit of beauty and joy which is the basic characteristic of this kingdom of life, and shares it with us. Reading this book, it is possible to learn a great deal about the abstract nature of the inner planes, the way in which light ensouls itself in form, and the intelligence and order of universal law—and yet be entertained and lifted up in spirit all the while.

The Real World of Fairies is a treasure.

The Space Trilogy
by C. S. Lewis

C.S. Lewis was an intense student of the nature of God and divine involvement in the affairs of mankind. As a professor at Cambridge University, he wrote many philosophical pieces on Christian ethics. But fortunately for us, he did not limit himself to scholarly writing. He also wrote several masterpieces of fiction, including *The Space Trilogy*.

This collection of novels is once again dramatic proof that fiction is often the best vehicle for treating the nature of good and evil, because the struggle between nobility and baseness is a vintage human struggle. In the hands of a master storyteller, it inevitably forms the basis of a gripping tale, as well as providing us with the opportunity to rehearse vicariously for our own struggles with evil.

The action begins in *Out of the Silent Planet*. Lewis's hero, Professor Ransom, is kidnapped by mad scientists Devine and Weston and taken to another planet. Once there, Ransom escapes and discovers that the focal point of civilized life on this planet is the presence of God. *Eldila*, which are something like angels, commonly appear to the human beings inhabiting the planet, speaking as agents of God.

In fact, the attitude of these people toward God differs remarkably from the attitudes prevailing on earth, which is known as "the silent planet" because God is unable to communicate directly to the unheeding earthlings. Ransom seizes the opportunity of being on this planet to explore the nature of God, first in discussions with the local inhabitants and then directly through his own experiences. In this way, Lewis adroitly weaves in his perspectives on the unity of life and the order of divine intelligence.

Knowing the reality and force of divine law, the people of this planet willingly cooperate with it. Knowing the purpose of God, they work to fulfill it. Knowing the power and benevolence of God, they trust their Creator fully.

Devine and Weston, representing the worst of ignorant materialism and godlessness in human society, stand in stark contrast. At the end of the novel, they are brought before the spiritual intelligence in charge of the planet. Confronting this great intelligence, the absurdity and pettiness of their evil nature is revealed.

In *Perelandra*, Ransom journeys to the planet of that name, where Weston is once more trying to find his fortune illicitly. The nature of Perelandra is unique. It is a new planet where death does not occur and the entire human race is a *single* Lady-Mother. Weston is possessed by an earth devil who cunningly employs all the propaganda, lies, and distortions he has learned on earth in an attempt to seduce the Eve-like Lady-Mother.

The dialogues between this devil and the Lady-Mother are quite possibly the finest in print on the nature of temptation and the rationalizations we use for defying the will of God. Some of the arguments the devil uses—the need to be self-sufficient, independent, and strong in order to overcome exploitation—strike exceedingly close to home in modern society.

In the final battle, Ransom almost exhausts his strength and sanity, and prays to God for deliverance. But in the end, he realizes that *he is the miracle* he prayed for—that God does work, but *through him*. This enables him to defeat the devil and discover that he has served the human race of this planet as Christ served the people on earth in His time. This struggle helps us appreciate that the nature of evil is often very subtle—and even attractive. In the hands of deceitful people, reason and logic can become tools of evil.

The final book of the trilogy, *That Hideous Strength*, takes place in modern England. A small group of university professors and scientists, embodying the principles of scientific pragmatism and logical positivism, set out to take over a university town, aided by the "hideous strength" of evil intelligences. The ultimate goal, of course, is to take over all of society, and the parallel with Nazi Germany is unmistakable. The arrogance and materialism of the group is striking as it strives to seize control by manipulating the press, intimidating the townspeople, and exploiting crises to gain acceptance of their tyrannical rule.

A small cadre of people led by Professor Ransom are aware of the evil at hand. With the help of a young clairvoyant woman, they struggle to contain and defeat the fascist forces. But their own resources are not enough, so they summon the presence of Merlin, the ancient magician of King Arthur's court, to help them in the fray. In this way, they are able to defeat the evil of the present day with magic from ancient times.

The Space Trilogy deserves to be acclaimed as a masterpiece of metaphysical fiction.

Eyes of Horus
by Joan Grant

Ra-ab is the son of the ruler of Oryx, one of the provinces of ancient Egypt. His childhood is a pleasant one, because the Oryx is at peace—and wisely ruled by his father. But such is not the case throughout the rest of Egypt.

The government and religion of this proud nation have been corrupted, taken over almost entirely by dark forces. No longer is Pharaoh a strong, divinely inspired leader; instead, he rules by fear and imposes unjust taxes. No longer is the temple a sanctuary of truth and light; the true religion has been usurped by the worship of Set, prince of the darkness. Indeed, many of the practices described are barbaric and savage—not only to us, but also to the sensibilities of Ra-ab and others like him.

Secretly, they have formed a group called "the watchers" or the "eyes of Horus," in reference to a major Egyptian deity. This group, which is dedicated to the overthrow of the system of government and the restoration of enlightened rule in Egypt, slowly builds its influence and size.

Ra-ab and his sister Kiyas are key figures in the revolution. Although they have not yet developed the intuitive powers of their mother, the inner life is very active in this story—especially in a dramatic confrontation between the priests of light and the priests of darkness.

Eyes of Horus is probably the most mature and exciting of all the Joan Grant "far memories"—novels based on her recollection of her own earlier lives.

Lord of the Horizon
by Joan Grant

The story of Ra-ab Hotep continues. The new Pharaoh, Amenemhet, put in power by the military victory of Ra-ab Hotep, has ignored his counsel. As a result, Pharaoh's son has become the object of court intrigue. At last, Amenemhet realizes Senusert will be unfit to rule unless his attitudes and training are drastically altered. He asks Ra-ab Hotep and his wife Meri-osis to take his son into their home and raise him.

The challenge is a great one, because Senusert has been spoiled by those who would use him to their own ends. But Ra-ab Hotep and his wife are equal to the task, and patiently work to help Senusert grow to maturity. They are frequently aided by their psychic abilities, which are highly developed, and by their deep understanding of karmic law and the purposes of human evolution.

In the end, the son learns his lessons better than his father, Amenemhet, who must struggle with the ghost of his murdered mother-in-law in one of the most bone-chilling descriptions of psychic attack in print. Once again, it is Ra-ab who comes to the aid of his friend and liberates him from the vengeance of the dead.

Like all Joan Grant books, *Lord of the Horizon* is marvelous reading—a "far memory" of life in ancient Egypt, liberally spiced with powerful insights into reincarnation, psychic experiences, the spiritualization of consciousness, the necessity of opposing evil with wisdom, enlightened leadership in government and religion, and kinship with life.

The Magic Kingdom of Landover
by Terry Brooks

In an attempt to escape a successful but boring life as an attorney, Ben Holiday buys Landover, a magic kingdom, for one million dollars. To his dismay, he gets what he paid for—and a whole lot more. But Ben's loss is our gain: a trio of action-packed, magical stories.

The first novel, *Magic Kingdom For Sale*, sets the scene. The kingdom is in ruin. The Barons refuse to recognize a king, and demons, a dragon, and an evil witch threaten the country. His entourage is small: an incompetent magician, a talking dog, and a tree. Even the Paladin, champion of the kings, seems to be just a myth.

Holiday, of course, proves to be a worthy king, and overcomes all these obstacles. Author Terry Brooks keeps the action moving breathlessly—so well, in fact, we might miss the story's subtleties.

In point of fact, the story is a marvelous allegory of the spiritual path. The real magic kingdom is the life of consciousness; we all have one within us, but mostly ignore it. Once we discover we have this inner kingdom, we enter the spiritual path. But like Holiday, we find it is not all fun and games. There are inner realities (the reluctant barons) who will not obey us. And there are emotional conditions (the river folk and fairies) which seem even more illogical and unruly.

At the end, almost exhausted, Holiday must face almost certain defeat—the chief demon (the dweller on the threshold). This proves too much, until the Paladin (the soul) comes to his rescue, endowing him with superhuman gifts. In this portrait of the third initiation, the story ends. The real magic kingdom is within us.

In the second novel, *The Black Unicorn*, Holiday loses control of the throne, as the result of being deluded by the evil wizard. In a stunning sequence of manipulation and deceit, the wizard convinces Ben that he is under a spell, which causes everyone except his enemies to mistake him for only a ragged laborer.

Ben struggles with this sudden loss of power and identity, but as the prism cat Dirk points out, it is only "magic of his own making" that has led to this dire condition.

Dirk is right. Ben, like every spiritual aspirant, must learn to discern between his own fantasies, wishes, and fears on the one hand and reality on the other. A clearsighted person can never be deceived.

Slowly, after many hints and much encouragement, Ben begins to understand how he has been tricked and what he must do to regain his authority. He realizes that he never lost the magic that he once had; he merely lost confidence in it. As the confidence returns, he is once more united with the full spiritual force of the Paladin, his knight-protector (the Soul). He subdues the opposition and restores the kingdom to peace and prosperity.

Fun to read, this second novel in the series is not only a high-spirited adventure story but also a first-rate textbook on the nature of illusion and how we deceive ourselves. It teaches us to discern between our concepts of truth and the power of truth itself—and how to dispel glamours and delusions without generating more.

Wizard at Large completes *The Magic Kingdom of Landover* series. In this novel, the old, evil king Michael Ard Rhi of Landover, now exiled to earth and living near Seattle, has loosed an evil force back in Landover, which may defeat the gentle king Ben and restore Michael to power.

The plot is set in motion by an untimely sneeze, just when the wizard is trying to free Abernathy, the court scribe who has been turned into a dog. But the real meaning of this tale unfolds at a deeper level, in a marvelous dramatization of the true magic of the human mind and emotions. In real life, threats, curses, pessimism, joy, and devotion are mostly intangible, and have mainly subjective effects. This novel uses poetic license to make them come alive in the form of a dragon (the fire-belching force of the undisciplined will) and by turning unspoken curses into tangible and objective manifestations.

In the end, cleverness, goodwill, and persistence turn out to be the most wonderful magic of all, and evil is defeated.

Every student of the human psyche and the spiritual path will enjoy and be enriched by these three books. *The Magic Kingdom of Landover* is not just fun to read, but it can also teach us a great deal about the magic of life.

Edgar Cayce on Reincarnation
by Noel Langley

Few topics are more controversial than reincarnation. The majority of people in the world believe in it; almost no one in the West does. Yet even among those who accept the doctrine, few understand it in its true esoteric sense. All too many embrace it as a stimulus to their fantasies or an excuse from their responsibilities.

There are a lot of books on this subject; the difficulty is finding one which treats reincarnation rationally and sensibly. The world does not need another gushing volume about lovers finding their "soul mates" or the alleged wonders of hypnotic regression as therapy. It needs a common sense approach that emphasizes the growth that occurs from life to life, and the responsibility that we incur to live life wisely and helpfully. This is the tone struck by Noel Langley in his examination of reincarnation and karma based on the Edgar Cayce readings, *Edgar Cayce on Reincarnation.*

Langley gives a thorough description of Cayce's readings and how his own perspective on reincarnation evolved through the years. But he does not limit himself to Cayce's work; he puts reincarnation in a historical perspective and draws freely from other sources as well. Liberally spiced with examples from the Cayce readings, this book not only helps us understand reincarnation but why it is important to us. It also presents a practical explanation of the workings of grace.

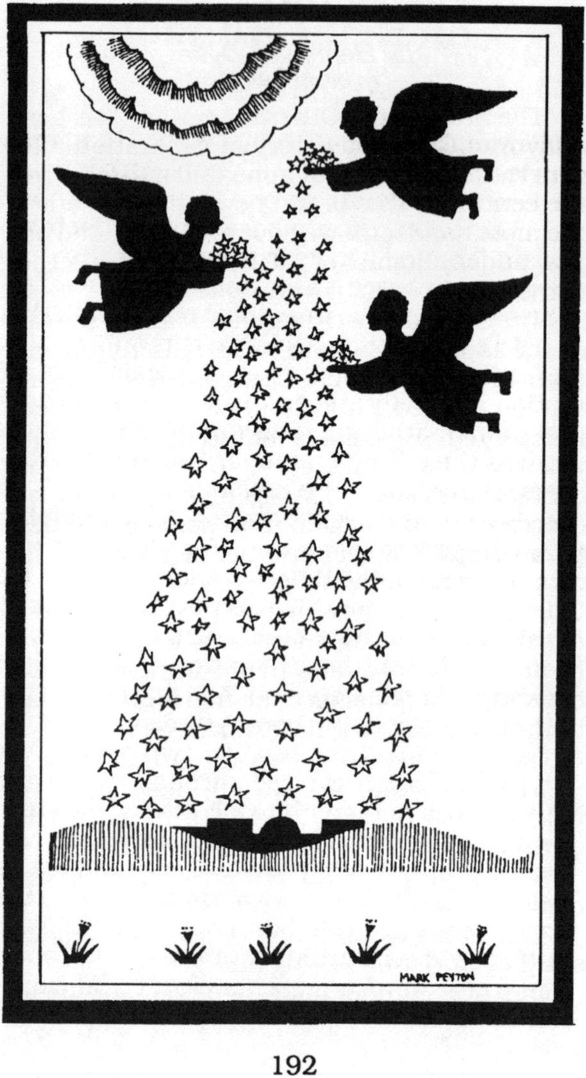
MARK PEYTON

The Story of the Other Wise Man
by Henry van Dyke

"The Story of the Other Wise Man" has been a favorite Christmas story of generation after generation since it first appeared at the turn of the century. This brand new edition is one of the most handsome we have ever seen, and has the added bonus of including three other Christmas stories by van Dyke.

"The Story of the Other Wise Man" is the tale of the fourth wise man, who fails to join his three brethren because he stops to help a dying traveler. Indeed, throughout his life, this pattern is repeated. His goal is to find the Christ, but whenever he comes close to making actual contact with Jesus, he is diverted from his dream by a cry for help from someone in desperate need. Time after time, he sacrifices his own dream in order to help those in need.

In the end, as he lies dying, he feels he has failed in his lifelong quest, only to realize that he has not failed at all. In putting the needs of others ahead of his own, he has found the key to the Christ life within his own heart.

The other stories in this edition are:

"The Christmas Angel," an imaginative retelling of how the angels came to announce the birth of Christ to the shepherds in the field.

"The Lost Word," a powerful story of the healing power of divine knowledge.

"The Spirit of Christmas," an essay on the spirit of Christmas living and giving.

This new edition makes a perfect gift book.

90 Days to Self-Health
by C. Norman Shealy, M.D.

C. Norman Shealy, M.D. is one of the most authoritative voices of the holistic health movement. He is a neurosurgeon who has spent the last 20 years exploring alternatives to surgery, especially in the control and healing of chronic pain. The result of this ongoing search is *90 Days to Self-Health*, which has become a classic in the field of holistic medicine. It presents, in common sense, easy-to-understand language, a complete program by which almost anyone can regain control of his or her physical and emotional health within just 90 days.

Dr. Shealy calls his program "Biogenics," which means "origin of life." It is his contention that health—both good and ill—does not just happen. It emerges from a combination of factors. Some of these factors, like genetic makeup, are beyond our control. But others, such as diet, lifestyle, work conditions, and emotional maturity, are very much under our control. And they can be changed, giving us a foundation for much better health.

This is not just a book of cobwebby theory, telling you that it can be done but failing to show you how. On the contrary, it is a practical, usable book chock full of practical exercises, affirmations, and suggestions. It guides you, step-by-step, through each of the 90 days of Shealy's program. It also helps you create your own program for self-health.

90 Days to Self-Health puts the tools for improved health in our hands. All we have to do is supply the determination.

Scarlet Feather

by Joan Grant

Piyanah is a girl born into an American Indian tribe that has lost its true heritage and has become the prey of prejudice and superstition. She grows up with her cousin Raki as outsiders to the tribe, because her mother refuses to accept the restrictions of tradition. But in truth, Piyanah is the daughter of the chief, and after her mother dies, her father selects both Piyanah and Raki to be his successors and form a new tribe, free of the superstitious past.

First, however, they must prove themselves. This results in a curious role reversal, as Piyanah must play the role of a young brave, and Raki is sent to live with the squaws. In this way, the tribe comes to accept them as joint leaders.

Once the tribe accepts them, however, they must still be accepted by the chiefs of the neighboring tribes. This spells trouble, for one of the heirs of another tribe refuses to accept Piyanah as an equal. In order to settle this dispute, Piyanah must earn a scarlet feather—the highest recognition a brave can earn. As it turns out, both she and Raki earn the scarlet.

Piyanah and Raki take the new generation which will form the core of their new tribe in search of new hunting grounds, where they can settle. This journey leads them into the American Rockies and apparently the area of the Salt Lake. They endure much hardship, but eventually reach a fertile valley where they can build their new tribe.

Scarlet Feather is a marvelous novel in the Joan Grant "far memory" series.

I Ching On Line
by Robert R. Leichtman, M.D. and Carl Japikse

The I Ching is an ancient Chinese system of philosophy that helps us understand the immutable workings of cosmic law and the spiritual principles of life. It can also be used to understand specific problems of our personal life and to help us make decisions concerning the right action to take in any situation.

I Ching On Line is a new presentation of the standard I Ching text, designed to be used either with an IBM PC computer or in the more traditional manner, with coins or yarrow sticks.

The key advance made by *I Ching On Line* is that the commentary is divided into four modules, each module designed to answer a specific kind of question—pertaining either to health, decision making, relationships, or growth.

The four books containing the commentaries are *Healing Lines, Ruling Lines, Connecting Lines*, and *Changing Lines.*

Authors Robert R. Leichtman, M.D. and Carl Japikse have not just translated the text of the I Ching—they have actually reinterpreted the archetypal forces each hexagram represents and restated their meanings for modern life situations in the West. The result is a fresh statement of the meaning of each hexagram.

Each book also contains a lengthy introduction in which the authors describe their approach to using the I Ching. It strips away the mystery and confusion which often surrounds the I Ching and makes the whole process of consulting this venerable oracle much more sensible and comprehensible.

The Place of the Lion
by Charles Williams

In a sleepy English village, a small group of aspirants begin an experiment in creating thought-forms that carry with them a fragment of the power of divine archetypes. Unfortunately, the experiment is flawed—some of the small band long for the power of the inner patterns, others are overwhelmed by divine beauty or love. But no one in control balances all three aspects of divinity—and so no one, in effect, is in control.

The results are terrifying—and threaten human existence on the planet. Strange beasts begin to appear—first, a lion that changes into a lioness, then huge butterflies, horses, and even a unicorn. The leader of the group is knocked unconscious by the lioness, and a breech is created between heaven and earth. Through this breech, all of mythology is coming into physical being, threatening to undo the holy command that man have dominion over all life on earth.

All is not lost, however, for our hero is a man of exceptional mental skills, able to grasp the severity of the situation from the beginning and take action to heal it. He becomes an incarnation of divine wisdom, blending love, power, and beauty within himself, and is thereby able to stanch the gap in creation itself.

Of course, the beasts are not meant to be actual animals—they each represent some facet of the dark side of human nature, the beast within us which must be tamed to reveal the light within us.

The Place of the Lion is a masterpiece.

Dance Band on the Titanic
by Jack L. Chalker

Jack Chalker is one of the best writers of esoteric science fiction today—stories that embody and reflect esoteric truths while stretching our imaginations and entertaining us with high adventure. He specializes in four- and five-volume sets of novels. So it is rare indeed to find *Dance Band on the Titanic,* a collection of shorter writings, primarily stories.

This collection has nothing to do with the historical *Titanic.* The title of the book comes from one of the stories, in which a ferry boat travels back and forth between several alternative worlds. The same people occupy each world, but their lives differ in each sphere. In one, America is still a British colony; in another, the South wins the Civil War. In this way, Chalker stretches our imagination to embrace several dimensions of time and space simultaneously.

"Stormsung Runner" is another fascinating story in which very ordinary people are in charge of producing varieties of weather—thunderstorms, warm days, hail, and blizzards. This puts unusual stress on them, but also gives us an unusual insight into the invisible intelligences which actually do direct the weather.

One of the most fascinating pieces is a nonfiction description of his own approach to writing, "Where Do You Get Those Crazy Ideas?" In it, for instance, he describes the origin of many of the key elements in his Well World novels.

This is a fascinating set of stories.

The Unobstructed Universe
by Stewart Edward White

For 20 years, Stewart and Betty White explored the inner dimensions of life. Betty would go into a mediumistic trance, allowing Stewart to communicate, either with her, as she observed some phenomenon of the inner life, or with one of the Invisibles who guided their explorations. They published the results of these investigations in two classic statements, *The Betty Book* and *Across the Unknown*.

When Betty died, it seemed to bring to an end their mutual explorations of the inner life. But this was not to be the case. Some months later, when Stewart was visiting their old friends Darby and Joan, Joan—who was an excellent medium herself—went into trance. The Invisible who came in to speak was none other than Betty.

This began a series of three dozen trance sessions in which Betty led Stewart and Darby on a whole new tour of the inner side of life—a tour of what she called "the unobstructed universe," now that she could examine it free of all the obstructions of our physical senses and earthly biases.

The result is *The Unobstructed Universe*, one of the most profound books on the inner life ever published. It is a lucid examination of the nature of consciousness and how we exist in time and space—and what this all means to our daily lives on earth.

The Unobstructed Universe is an example of mediumship at its finest.

The Philosopher's Stone
by Colin Wilson

The philosopher's stone is a magical substance believed by alchemists to have the power to change base metal into gold. To Colin Wilson, the real philosopher's stone is the human mind with all its unlimited potential.

The Philosopher's Stone is quite possibly Wilson's most exciting adventure novel—an adventure by two scientists into the far reaches of the human imagination and awareness. The journey begins with the recognition that most people waste their lives on trivia, limited by habit and convention—and with an undaunted urge to go beyond these limits and awaken the real potential of the mind.

This they do, tapping higher dimensions of perception and intuition—and the ability to drink in insights at the abstract levels of the mind. Using their new powers, the scientists begin to search for insight into what has held back the development and use of human intelligence. This leads them to discover "the Old Ones"—dormant but immensely powerful beings who created much of the life on the planet.

This book is a true joy to read. It contains one of the finest descriptions of psychometry in print, and brilliant insights into the unique value of the will-to-know and the will-to-love. As Wilson says, he leaves to other writers the challenge to make people feel emotions; in his opinion, we feel too often and think too little.

It is the intent of *The Philosopher's Stone* to make us think—and it succeeds. It is one of the finest novels of our age.

The Winged Bull

by Dion Fortune

Dion Fortune wrote many of the finest esoteric novels presently available. *The Winged Bull* is one of the most powerful of them all.

The title refers to an ancient esoteric cult, the Winged Bull, which had its origins in Assyria. Two different groups of magicians, one set white and the other set black, accidentally invoke the power of this ancient cult, while trying to tap the secret powers of magic.

What draws the two groups together in conflict is that they are both trying to use the same person, a young woman named Ursula, as their primary channel with the Winged Bull. The black magicians are trying to dominate and enslave Ursula at an inner level; the white magicians, led by her half brother Brangwyn, are trying to heal her vulnerability to the others and liberate her from their grasp. Thrust into the middle of this power struggle is the hero of the novel, Ted Murchison, who ultimately must rescue Ursula from her entanglement in black magic and lead her through her ordeal.

The Winged Bull is a strong novel of human sexuality and the magical forces which influence the lives of all of us. It is also a brilliant portrayal of how ancient psychic and magical forces can still be alive and potent in the present day, and should be invoked and handled only by those who are trained in doing so.

It is also an absorbing recreation of the true power of magic. Ultimately, it is the esoteric force of magic itself that is the true hero and the most finely drawn "character" of this novel.

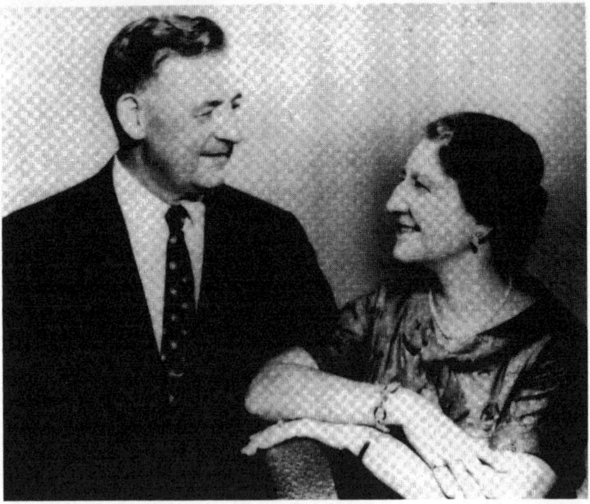

The Gift of Healing
by Ambrose & Olga Worrall

"The great healing power of the Holy Spirit is around us and available to us in church, in our homes, in a taxicab or a gasoline station or a hospital room—wherever the need is, one can reach out to this power. If we cannot touch the undying flame, we can, in any case, draw near its Divine warmth that reshapes and rebuilds and restores."

So write Ambrose and Olga Worrall in *The Gift of Healing*, a remarkable chronicle of their life experiences as the two best-known spiritual healers in America. It is a story of hope and the healing power of spiritual love—probably the best personal story of healing in print today.

Ambrose and Olga Worrall were responsible for the healing of thousands of people through the use of their gift over a fifty-year period. In addition, Olga founded the New Life Clinic in Baltimore and participated in dozens of scientific experiments that proved beyond any doubt that spiritual healing does work and can produce amazing results.

This new, memorial edition includes a moving afterword by Robert R. Leichtman, M.D., who served on the healing team of the New Life Clinic with Olga. *The Gift of Healing* is an exciting book to read, not only for its genuine insights into healing, but also for the descriptions of the Worralls' psychic abilities. It leads us into new understanding.

As the Worralls put it, "Spiritual healing, like all healing, is only a technique for achieving wholeness, and all wholeness is of God."

The Screwtape Letters
by C. S. Lewis

Screwtape is an accomplished devil, an expert at tempting humans and causing them to fall from grace. Wormwood is his nephew—a "junior tempter"—whom Screwtape has taken under his wing, to educate in the fine art of seduction. The result is a series of letters from Screwtape to Wormwood which deserves to be considered a modern masterpiece of both satire and human behavior.

For even though the protagonists of this story are demons, the real subjects are humans trying to come to terms with who they are—one human being in particular, who has been assigned to Wormwood as his "client."

Letter after letter, Screwtape instructs Wormwood in the weaknesses of human nature—self-deception, hypocrisy, pettiness, and selfishness. He exhorts Wormwood to keep his client diverted from a real understanding of "the Enemy"—God—and suggests all manner of ways to do so. In the process, Lewis neatly uses the cutting edge of humor to slice through popular beliefs about attitude and emotion and demonstrate the subtle, thoughtless ways we tempt ourselves—and succumb.

The Screwtape Letters is witty and delightful, a tongue-in-cheek dramatization of the struggle between darkness and light. And even though the author plays humorously off the idea of a devil, it becomes clear that our real struggle is not with some laughable demon, but with the seeds of ignorance and selfishness within our own character.

Masters and Men

by Virginia Hanson

One of the most remarkable phenomena of the early days of Theosophy was the correspondence which occurred between A.P. Sinnet and two of the Masters, Koot Hoomi and Morya.

Sinnet was a journalist who met H.P. Blavatsky soon after her arrival in India, following the publication of *Isis Unveiled*. Impressed by the materialization of messages from the Masters, he asked her to forward a letter of his own to them. To his surprise, an answer materialized in his locked room several days later—and thus the correspondence began.

The actual letters from the Masters to Sinnet are a historical fact, on display in the British Museum. But the letters themselves do not convey the whole story behind this unique correspondence—the story of Madame Blavatsky, Sinnet, H.S. Olcott, and the tumultuous formative years of the Theosophical Society.

Wanting to retell this story, author Virginia Hanson chose to take the actual facts and documents and assemble them in the form of a narrative. The result is *Masters and Men*, a novel focusing on the interaction between the superphysical masters and the very human men and women who served as their agents.

This is not just a story for those with an interest in the early days of Theosophy. It is a story of importance to all spiritual aspirants, because it reveals how difficult it is to bring new ideas into human awareness—and how important the guidance of our "Elder Brothers" is.

Masters and Men is highly recommended.

The Razor's Edge
by W. Somerset Maugham

"The sharp edge of a razor is difficult to pass over; thus the wise say the path to Salvation is hard." With this quote from the Upanishads as his motto, Somerset Maugham begins his stirring novel of self-discovery and enlightenment, *The Razor's Edge*. It is a novel of a group of friends who repeatedly cross paths in different locales throughout the world, as they sample the pleasures and sorrows of Experience.

The focal point of the story is Larry, who seeks to give his experiences meaning. But it is not just Larry who attempts to walk on the razor's edge—it is actually every character: Elliott, the snob; Isabel, the socialite; Gray, the "regular guy"; Suzanne, the artist's model; and Sophie, lost in wantonness. They continually jab their feet and suffer the consequences.

Overtly, they learn very little from their experiences—except Larry. Larry takes his confusion seriously. He travels to India to find someone who can enlighten him. After many disappointments, he finally locates an ashram. He stays there for two years, until he realizes that enlightenment comes from wise living, not withdrawal into solitary contemplation.

So he returns to Paris and reenters the web of relationships spun by his friends. But he is free of the assumptions and limitations that cripple his friends. He moves through life with a grace they observe, but cannot duplicate.

The Razor's Edge is a powerful novel, full of insight into the duality of human reactiveness and what it means to harmonize it.

Lord of Light
by Roger Zelazny

The conflict between matter and spirit is an eternal struggle, obvious to any intelligent person who observes his own life or events in society. Theology, sociology, psychology, and philosophy deal with this conflict on their own terms. But in many ways, this struggle is best explored through good fiction.

This is exactly what Roger Zelazny's *Lord of Light* does. Condensing the many facets of the eternal battle into a few symbolic themes, Zelazny skillfully weaves them into a tapestry of plot, myth, heroism, cowardice, destruction, and triumph. The story takes place on another planet in the far future. A few men have set themselves up as gods, borrowing freely from the Hindu pantheon, and control the world with technological mastery.

Through their machinations and advanced science, they stifle progress and create an intellectual dark age. But the Lord of Light, known as Maitreya and as Buddha, opposes them, not with superior technical power but with his philosophy and teaching, which exposes the hypocrisy and lust of the "gods" while liberating the people.

Quoting the book, "Death and Light are everywhere, always, and they begin, end, strive, attend into and upon the Dream of the Nameless that is the world, burning words within Samsara, perhaps to create a thing of beauty."

Zelazny's creation of beauty gives new life to rich Hindu myths, in a fascinating clash between light and darkness.

Assignment in Eternity

by Robert Heinlein

What could possibly be better than a story by Robert Heinlein, the greatest science fiction writer of this century?

Four stories by Robert Heinlein.

That is precisely what *Assignment in Eternity* delivers—two novellas and two short stories. Combined, they are guaranteed to take you into dimensions you have never entered before. The journey is worth it, even if you have to give up some excess baggage along the way, such as preconceived ideas about space and time.

Gulf is a tale about the gap or gulf that separates humans from their rich inner potential. A superspy gets drawn into a sequence of events which lead him to develop his full thinking capacity—and save humanity.

Elsewhen is a classic short story about the disappearance of a group of students of "speculative metaphysics," who discover how to step into other time tracks and choose not to return to the one they left.

In *Lost Legacy*, a similar group of intrepid explorers of the inner dimensions stumble on a Shangri-la in the Shasta Mountains, where they find the missing satirist Ambrose Bierce still alive—and other surprises, too!

The final story is *Jerry Was A Man*, a clever tale about the evolution of an anthropoid into a thinking, feeling man—with a sharp, swift kick of an ending.

The next time you depart for the fourth or fifth dimensions, be sure to take *Assignment in Eternity* with you!

A Search in Secret India
by Paul Brunton

Paul Brunton was one of the great husbandmen who toiled in the fields of humanity, sowing the seeds of spirituality in the West during the first half of this century, so that we might reap the harvest now that the century is ending. Trained as a journalist, he traveled widely through India and Egypt, learning their spiritual traditions. He then devoted his life to sharing what he had learned in a series of books.

A Search in Secret India was the first of these books to appear, and it remains today one of the most fascinating and enlightening books available on the Eastern traditions of spiritual growth. It is the highly entertaining report of Brunton's travels and experiences in seeking out, talking, and studying with some of the most colorful spiritual figures of India fifty years ago—genuine saints and first-class fakes.

At times, the narrative stretches the Western imagination, because some of the feats described defy our present understanding. But Brunton never overrates these phenomena. He knows that the true power of spirit lies in awareness, not magic, and continually seeks out the true presence of the light within. More often than not, he finds it—and we do, too.

As the *London Times* said, "His work is excellent. It has life, color, movement. Readers will find their interest unflagging from the first page to the last." Indeed, the search leads Brunton to his teacher, and spiritual unfoldment. It has the power to help others in the same way, too.

The Autobiography of a Yogi

by Paramahansa Yogananda

Unquestionably the one teacher who has done the most to bring the light of the spiritual East to the attention of the West is Paramahansa Yogananda. Born in India in 1893, he dedicated himself to the spiritual life at a young age, studying in the ashram of Sri Yukteswar while also pursuing more conventional studies.

Yogananda grew quickly into spiritual adulthood; in 1920, he was chosen to represent India as a delegate to the International Congress of Religious Liberals in Boston. This was the beginning of his work in America, which lasted until his death in 1952.

For 10 years, Yogananda traveled extensively throughout the United States, lecturing and teaching the principles of Kriya Yoga. In the 1930's, he shifted his focus, teaching primarily at the Self-Realization Fellowship.

Yet *The Autobiography of a Yogi* is much more than the story of an enlightened man's life. It is almost a "cook's tour" of spiritual India, filled with personal reminiscences of this saint and that guru. It is a story of miraculous events and unexplainable phenomena—and yet it is introduced with a quote from John 4:48: "Except ye see signs and wonders, ye will not believe."

Indeed, Yogananda thought himself as much a disciple of Jesus as any guru, and in this book strives to blend the Christian with the Hindu, so that we may see the light behind, and within, both.

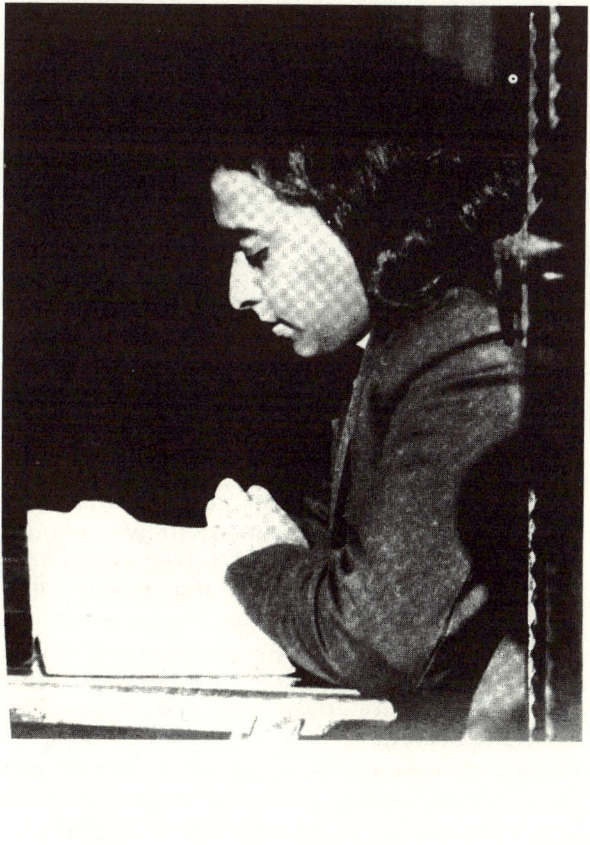

Job: A Comedy of Justice
by Robert Heinlein

The intense emphasis on suffering as a part of the "religious life" is one of the most bizarre legacies of Judeo-Christian theology. Why would a benevolent God take delight in the hardships of His followers, or even those who reject Him?

In order to answer this question, Robert Heinlein decided to go to the source—the source, in this case, being the book of Job in the Old Testament—and rewrite it in modern terms. The result is a delicious concoction of satire, philosophy, humor, and adventure.

The new Job is a fellow named Alex who is chief fundraiser for a large fundamentalist church. He and his wife Margaret suffer tribulation after tribulation. Each time, just as they are about to triumph over adversity, Yahweh (the God of the Old Testament) changes the rules, and their suffering begins anew.

Finally, Alex makes it to heaven, but has been separated from Margaret. To him, this is as bad as hell, so he demands to go there. In hell, he finds that unlike Yahweh, the Devil does not make his chosen suffer. In fact, it is pretty nice.

This leads to a cosmic confrontation, in which the Devil exposes Yahweh's preoccupation with suffering to the true God, and justice is finally served. In this way, the hypocrisy of fundamentalist and Old Testament theology is exposed, making it clear that God is indeed benevolent and just, not wrathful and bigoted, as the fundamentalists are.

Job is a funny, thought-provoking book.

The Four Lords of the Diamond
by Jack Chalker

The Diamond is a group of four planets that serve as an intergalactic penal colony for criminals unwilling to reform—a very effective prison indeed, since anyone sent to one of these planets is infected by an organism which will kill him if he leaves the Diamond.

This arrangement works well, until it is discovered that powerful alien beings have entered into a secret alliance with the four lords of the Diamond to use these planets as a staging area for an invasion of all other planets in the region.

To combat this threat, secret agents are sent to each of the four planets to search out the overlord of that world, assassinate him, take his place, and find out about the aliens and their plans. These agents are controlled mentally by an Agent With No Name who stays safely outside the Diamond. The exploits of each agent form one of the four novels in this new tetralogy by Jack Chalker. Each book is named after one of the planets:

Lilith: A Snake in the Grass.
Cerberus: A Wolf in the Fold.
Charon: A Dragon at the Gate.
Medusa: A Tiger by the Tail.

These four books are a feast of adventure that builds to a startling climax, as the true identity of the aliens is revealed. In addition, all four are filled with fascinating descriptions of psychic phenomena and highly accurate simulations of the etheric and astral planes.

The Apprentice Adept
by Piers Anthony

Stile has a problem. He exists in two worlds at the same time. One of the worlds, Proton, is scientific, materialistic, and environmentally ruined; life there can exist only in domed cities. The other world, Phaze, is a natural paradise where magic rules, instead of science.

Proton is governed by a small number of very wealthy citizens, while the bulk of the population, like Stile, are serfs. Phaze is loosely governed by powerful adepts of magic, whom most of the population fear.

Many of the people in Proton also exist in the magical world of Phaze, although few recognize this fact. In addition to people, Proton has intelligent robots with human-like emotions and self-will. Phaze, by contrast, has golems—magical creatures formed out of wood and animated by the Brown Adept. Even more intriguing is the fact that Proton has horses while Phaze has magical unicorns that are capable of shifting into human shapes and intellects.

At first, Stile does not realize that he exists in both worlds, but he learns soon enough. For some reason, someone on Proton is trying to kill him. He escapes only because a robot helps him slip into Phaze through the "curtain" that separates the worlds.

Escaping into Phaze does not alleviate Stile's problems, however. On the contrary, he soon discovers that his alternate self on Phaze has already been murdered by sorcery—and he is due to be the next victim.

The three novels in Piers Anthony's marvelous

series, *The Apprentice Adept*, chronicle the story of Stile as he shuttles from Proton to Phaze and back again, always one step ahead of his assassin. The story begins in *Split Infinity*, becomes more entangled in *Blue Adept*, and is finally resolved in *Juxtaposition*.

As the story unfolds, Stile realizes that his only hope is to master each of the two worlds. On Proton, this means competing in the Great Games—Olympic-like games in which the single winner is given the status of citizen and immense wealth. On Phaze, it means Stile must become an adept and master its magical forces.

Working with this premise, Anthony spins a marvelous and exciting allegory of our own existence and spiritual challenges. Like Stile, each of us lives in two worlds—the physical and the astral—simultaneously, even though we usually do not recognize it. The physical is very much like Proton, while the astral is stunningly like Phaze.

Also like Stile, each of us is challenged to become spiritual masters of the worlds we live in. To achieve this, however, we must overcome not only all manner of opposition but also a broad gamut of temptation. In this regard, there is a great deal we can learn from Stile.

Gradually, Stile realizes it would be deadly to succumb to the ever-present temptation to use these "worldly ways." Instead, he commits himself to wage the battle without compromising his integrity.

The Apprentice Adept is a feast of entertainment, rich in insight into the human condition. Reading these novels has a magical way of helping us see our own lives from a more mature view.

Bestselling Titles

1. The Brotherhood of Angels and Men.
2. I Say Sunrise.
3. A Soul's Journey.
4. No One Hears But Him.
5. Winged Pharaoh.
6. The Impersonal Life.
7. Scars of the Soul.
8. The Secret Path.
9. Glory Road.
10. The Mind Parasites.
11. The Finding of the Third Eye.
12. Healing and Regeneration through Color and Music.
13. Practical Mysticism.
14. The Real World of Fairies.
15. Health and Light.
16. The Boy Who Saw True.
17. Divine Healing of Mind and Body.
18. Om, The Secret of Ahbor Valley.
19. Thought-Forms.
20. The Power of the Rays and Colour Meditations.
21. Far Memory.
22. After We Die, What Then?
23. An Illustrated Encyclopedia of Symbols.
24. The Seven Human Temperaments.
25. The Secret Teachings of All Ages.
26. The Reappearance of the Christ.
27. Narcissus and Goldmund.
28. Active Meditation.
29. The Earthsea Trilogy.
30. The Light Within Us.
31. The Gift of Healing.
32. The Bach Flower Remedies.